Would you like a FREE Story Bundle?

Includes downloadable story, recipe from Chapter 34, and playful printable from *Peeling Your Onion* - the workbook inspired from this book!

Go to https://heidiesther.com/bookbundle1 and *grab it!*

FOR CRYIN' OUT LOUD

HEIDI ESTHER

First Edition March 2022

Publisher's Cataloging-in-Publication data

Names: Esther, Heidi, author.

Title: For cryin' out3 loud : one mommy's journey to waking up, believing, and speaking up for her joy, complete with potty breaks! / by Heidi Esther.

Description: Champaign, IL: Joyfully Ever After Media, 2022.

Identifiers: ISBN 978-1-957225-01-2 (paperback)
| 978-1-957225-00-5 (ebook) | 978-1-957225-02-9 (audio)

Subjects: LCSH Esther, Heidi. | Mothers--United States--Biography. | Lesbian mothers--United States--Biography. | Dysfunctional families--United States. | Self-actualization (Psychology). | BISAC BIOGRAPHY & AUTOBIOGRAPHY / LGBTQ+ | BIOGRAPHY & AUTOBIOGRAPHY / Personal Memoirs | FAMILY & RELATIONSHIPS / Dysfunctional Families | BODY, MIND & SPIRIT / Inspiration & Personal Growth

Classification: LCC HQ755.86 E88 2022 | DDC 306.874/3--dc23

Cover design by Gentiana Keka
Editing by Sarah D. Moore
Interior design by Shabbir Hussain
Audio engineering by Denis Rykov

For information on bulk purchases,
please email howdy@heidiesther.com.

Printed in the United States of America

DEDICATION

*This book is dedicated to every soul
who falls down the rabbit hole.
Keep waking up, finding yourself,
and you will find your Muchness.*

Because you are worth more than Spanx.*

*In case you are not familiar with Spanx, think beige shiny 1980's workout shorts with a corset top that reaches just below your bosom.

To note

The following is my story from a baker's dozen years ago, and the feelings and events that happen are told to the best of my high standards of integrity and middle-aged brain. Some of the people in this book have different names. Because this is my truth.

PREFACE

A story from May 21, 2020

You would think that getting fired right before the pandemic is the worst thing. Especially with kids and a stay-at-home spouse to support.

Then, I bet you would think that two failed attempts at trying to find a new job would be even worse. Especially when they each took over forty hours to prep. From cover letter to networking to researching to identifying my values, I did it all. And topped it off with two exhausting eight-hour Zoom interviews.

And you would think both of those events would be cause for pandemic happy hours, also known as a day drinking. But you would be mistaken.

I woke up today. Actually, let me rephrase.

Someone woke me up in the middle of the night. For the seventh day in a row. And gave me the keys to something. Something that was standing right in front of me, like my face in the mirror. Only, I didn't see it until today.

Sanity.

For the past seven nights, I woke up between two and four am with this Sanity word in my brain. The first few days, I surprised and impressed myself with my extensive swear-cabulary at such an hour. I am a woman who prizes sleep above eating. Especially after years with toddlers.

As the days wore on, I noticed something else going on in my brain. Each time I woke, no matter the time, I felt like hopping out of bed. Yep, you heard that right. I felt as jubilant as Maria at the top of the Austrian Alps.

Sanity. The word rang. And rang. So, I tried a new tactic. I bargained for more sleep in a new way.

"Yes, I have Sanity. Yes, I love being home with my grumpy teenagers who can't see their friends, my dogs on anxiety meds, and my miserable, introverted partner in our small open-concept home. Thank you, *whoever* or *whatever* you are, for letting me notice how grateful I am." I said, to myself.

But even gratitude didn't work.

So, on the seventh day, today, I did something different. I woke up at four-thirty, got out of bed, and wrote. And a miracle happened. I unlocked my joy.

Hi, my name is Heidi Esther. I am a midwestern momma on my life's mission to guide you to your joy. More specifically, your Joyfully Ever After. No, I'm not a paramedic or a doctor. But, after forty-four years of breathing, I can look back and see every single step of the procedure that got me from avoidant doormat to joyful human.

And that's the gift I'm giving to you with my book. And my companion workbook, *Peeling Your Onion*. And through my true stories, self-reflections, playful printables at HeidiEsther.com. And through my authentic, empowering conversations I share on my **YouTube Channel, Pod,** and

The My Joyfully Ever After Facebook Group. Also through all the fun I have with Heather Kokx, awesome human, on our **YouTube Show** and **Facebook Group**, both by the name *Live with Heidi and Heather.*

So, back to you. Are you ready for your key to your joy? Great! Let's get started.

I think it makes sense to start at the beginning of the shitstorms, don't you think?

TABLE OF CONTENTS

INTRO

What healthy fruit or vegetable is hollow on the inside? No pit, no seeds, nothing. Visualize that you take out your knife to cut through it. Your hand puts pressure on the handle, assuming it will take some effort. Then, whunk! The knife jumps through a dead space and smacks the cutting board.

Can you think of what fruit or vegetable is hollow on the inside?

Okay, while you ponder, I'm going to talk to you about two other foods. Onions and parfaits. Not together, of course. We'll save Onion Parfaits for a page in another book, perhaps *National Geographic's 234 of the World's Weirdest Foods* for your neighborhood eight-year-old.

And, to be clear, this is not a cookbook. Though if you want my mom's authentic Swedish Meatball recipe referenced in Chapter 34, it's part of the companion workbook. Dare I say it's better than IKEA's meatballs? Yes, I do.

Let's first talk about onions.

A gregarious smile, chunky glasses, and wild wavy brown hair greet me as I walk into a local church lobby. The casual living room furniture and benches are pushed aside. Enough room for half a dozen yoga mats and humans.

Soon I'm laying on the floor. My eyes are closed. My yoga teacher starts the class.

"It's a little crowded today, ladies. So if you touch, don't be creepy about it. Take a deep breath. And start to peel through the layers of you that relate to everyone else. Like you take off your hat and shoes, peel through the layers of you that relate to your family and friends, your work. Until you come to You relating to You."

I visualize myself like an onion. Yes, partly because I like Shrek. I take off all my layers and my responsibilities, but I encounter a problem.

There's nothing on the inside. I've sliced right through dead air. I'm an onion with no inside. No me that I know.

That empty onion was who I was in the beginning of this story I am about to share with you. Here were all the layers of my parfait

- Mommy
- Wife
- Daughter
- Meticulous House Cleaner
- Reluctant Cook
- Volunteer

By the end of the story I have grown an inside to my onion.

Did you guess the hollow fruit or vegetable yet? Don't worry, I'm going to tell you. But next, let's move on to something tastier. Parfaits.

Who doesn't like a parfait?

Mmm. Mmm. All those creamy cool layers. Can you taste that ice cream hitting your tongue like a smooth after-wave caressing the shore? And not to be outdone, how do you like your next spoonful of whipped cream and hot fudge? The dynamic duo of light and rich?

What if your feelings were like the layers in your parfait? And as you walked around you had new layers added all the time. Which makes sense, right? Because we humans experience new feelings all the time.

If they were positive feelings, you would gobble up that tasty layer. Yet if they were shameful feelings, you might ignore your parfait altogether.

Do you see the problem here?

Say you got passed over for a promotion for the third time. You might have a giant layer of anger added right on top of your parfait. Now, if you decide to ignore your parfait because "you're fine," the anger isn't going to go away. Your parfait will still keep having layers added. And then, before you know it, you're lugging around a twenty-pound parfait with only salted peanuts. Your least favorite.

At the start of the story, I did not know I was carrying around the twenty-pound peanut parfait.

By the end of the story, I had noticed my feelings. And perhaps more importantly, I learned to accept them and ingest them. If you must know, it was a lot of nuts. But, for the first time in my life, I felt liberated. I held my head high as I walked around with a regular-sized parfait.

The answer to my first question

Did you come up with the answer to the question of *What healthy fruit or vegetable is hollow on the inside?* No seeds. No pit. Nothing?

GardeningKnowHow.com has an answer. Hollow fruit gets too much or too little water or nutrients. Or it was inadequately pollinated. Same with vegetables.

So there you go, there is no hollow healthy fruit or vegetable. Only unhealthy ones.

And so it is with people. And so it was with me.

May the following story inspire you to laugh and take steps toward discovering your healthy and true Inner Onion. And may you know you are brave enough to eat all the layers of your Feelings Parfait. If you want a guide to your Inner Onion and your Feelings Parfait, check out my companion workbook on Amazon.

For now, enjoy the show.

PART ONE

THE
RABBIT HOLE

CHAPTER 1

Driving Miss Daisy

November 17, 2009

The familiar shooting, piercing, boom of his voice echoes through my body and the minivan like an unwelcome firework.

"Did you hear what I said?" Mark continues, gathering momentum, his words like nails. "I. Had. To. Leave. Your. Son. To. Get. The. Groceries. It's His fault."

They were only in Meijer for 20 minutes. Wait. He left our son? What?

I can't say anything as I buckle into Miss Daisy, after getting my daughter's two-year shots. Miss Daisy is my royal blue minivan. I found a fake orange daisy one day at the self-service car wash and BOOM. Miss Daisy was born.

Yeah, I'm only 33, though most days I feel 80. So the shoes, er, tires, fit.

I look over at my husband of eight years, my dark curly-haired college match. His face is plum red, half-illuminated in the orange parking lot light. Hazel eyes oil-black, dilated, ready for battle. With who? I turn around, my three-year-old son's lower lip is trembling. Our son is right there. Oh God, I hope he didn't drag him by the arm again. That's so embarrassing. I shake my head, like trying to tamp out the fireworks.

"So, what happened exactly?" I ask.

"Go ahead, Jonathan, tell Mommy what you did," Mark says, turning the keys in the ignition and shooting more fireworks.

Silence in the backseat. My stomach sinks into a solid eight-ball. Mark pulls out of the parking lot, the orange parking lot lights flickering on his face.

"He wouldn't leave the blood pressure machine in the pharmacy section. So, I just left him there. I told him to stay. But, nooooo, he didn't listen. A store clerk found him and brought him to me."

Great, now I'm so irritated I won't be able to eat the only dinner that I've perfected: Campbell's-cheezy-chicken-broccoli-rice casserole.

As Mark speeds up on the main road home, I feel my body grinding to a halt like my VCR tape slowly getting caught up in the head mechanism. Dull, heavy. My hands are unable to stop clenching my 70's brown canvas (can it even be retro-cool if it's a) diaper bag. Are you fucking kidding me? Visions of child abductions run through my head. An eternity of silence ticks by under the orange glow of the street lights.

I feel some dark, looming presence with me. In the shadows. I feel like something is coming to get me. I brace for impact. Movement catches the side of my eye, and I hold my breath. I see flashes of red.

"Daddy! I got sticker and chippies!"

24

Whew. Barbie, my two-year-old, is waving her arms high in her red wool coat. Like she won the lottery. My body fog starts to lift. I look over to the mad driver, his face softening from the comment.

"The doctor gave you chippies?" Mark looks and adjusts the rearview mirror to look at our unsinkable, unflappable sprite of a daughter.

"Mommy gave me chippies! I did a poo-poo!"

Potty training. Though I will admit, *Lays* are hard to keep unbroken in diaper bags. My blonde Barbie is one savory girl. M&Ms don't work for her like for her older brother.

A small chuckle emanates from the driver's seat. The storm is past, but I can't just let Mark get away with this. He almost lost our son. And, equally important, how am I going to smooth this over?

We pull in from the gravel alley to our house in the middle of our midwestern college town. Our starter house is built like an early 1900's farmhouse. I call it The Farmhouse. It's old with updates. A perfect marriage. Like mine. Well, maybe.

Honestly, neither Mark nor I want to fix anything. Yes, yes, even though we both went to school to be engineers, we're more like soft-handed engineers. But I never practiced engineering anyway; I'm more of a non-profit girl – following my heart with an empty pocketbook. But that's a whole other story.

The downside of the house is that every winter, the frigid wind seeps through our plaster and lath walls and makes me wear my hat indoors. Too bad I can't saran wrap the walls.

It has white siding with dark magenta fake shutters. Seriously, why do people bother? It has two stories, and a basement that's shorter than I am. Which sucks because the laundry is down there, and I'm the only parent who fits. AND the first time it rained it flooded and ruined my preserved wedding dress. Why do they preserve those in boxes like they embalm dead people? I will admit, my white embroidered bust staring at me while I laundered diapers was creepy.

The high beige walls and black appliances of our kitchen meet me when we walk in the door. After we take off our snow boots, we walk through the dining room and toy room to the upstairs. The high ceilings, light hardwood, and curved hobbit-style openings feel like home to me.

We sit down at the dining room table. I buckle in Barbie, and Jonathan climbs in his booster seat all by himself. He's growing up so fast, but he still can't spell his name or tell people what his phone number is if he gets lost . . .

I clench my teeth. Let's just get this over with. I cut and plate the casserole. Mark first, then I keep three plates in front of me. On two of them, I spread out the casserole and start blowing on it. Time to start smoothing things over. I look up at Mark, and begin.

"So, how was your day?" I look back down, continue blowing, waiting to see if there will be another storm at dinner.

Mark munches on some cheesy-broccoli-goodness, focused on his plate. His face relaxes. Thank God.

"Actually, it was great. I think I'm going to get a holiday bonus this year. And they are going to put me in charge of a few young engineers. I mean, I thought they might pick David. But honestly, he doesn't have the people skills, like me."

Seriously? People skills? The man who can't keep track of his own son now has to keep track of grown adults? I hope they know what their phone numbers are. I stop blowing and hand the kids their plates. Breathe, Heidi. You want to enjoy dinner, right?

"Okay, wow. Well, that's terrific," I say. "Everyone, let's clap for Daddy. He did a great job today!"

A round of boisterous applause erupts from the table. Mark beams. I restrain myself from shaking my head. How come he gets the applause after almost losing his son?

Five minutes later we're all done but Barbie, who savors every bite. Mark leaves the table for his nightly kid-play-time with Jonathan. Barbie is done 25 minutes later, and it's time to kick my kid-nighttime routine into high gear. Bath. Check. Book time in Barbie's room. Today is the 300th-303rd telling of *Professor Wormbog in Search for the Zipperump-a-Zoo.*

Honestly, my favorite place in our house is Barbie's room upstairs. It's a converted attic with one tiny little window and sloped ceilings on both sides, right off our small, converted bedroom. It's painted a light orange that doesn't yell at you. When we moved in, it was already updated with laminate flooring and a western-facing window. The best part is that it's the warmest place in the house; when the kids are old, it will be mine.

The only thing I don't like about Barbie's room is her new Dora toddler bed. Ever since we got rid of the crib, she has been relishing her newfound freedom, by apparating right next to my face, in the middle of the night. No words, no sound. I *feel* this presence at 3am. I open my eyes, and I see this tiny Poltergeist-Carol-Ann stare back at me from five inches away. Creepy.

I tuck Barbie in and carry Jonathan across the hall to his big-boy room. He has a navy and white Tonka-Truck room. Why did I decorate it this way? He never plays with vehicles. I think I'm still irritated. I need to calm down so I go brew my old standby, coffee. The smell alone loosens the eight-ball in my stomach. How can coffee wake me up *and* calm me down? Weird.

I walk back upstairs. Now, what can I do while thinking over what happened? The linen closet it is. In 60 minutes I have refolded, trimmed, and weeded out any stray towels with frayed edges. I feel so much better, like when I finish rotating toys or put all my daughter's plastic barrettes back in their color-coded space on the ribbon.

I hear movement behind me, and my stomach returns to its eight-ball position, ready for another rumble.

"What are you doing?" Mark says.

I don't have strength for this. I quickly whip the drawer open and start changing into pjs.

"I'm straightening out the closet." I manufacture a yawn. "I'm gonna hit the hay. G'night."

Caught off-guard, Mark says, "Oh, umm, well, have a good night. I'm gonna watch some SportsCenter."

He throws on his Bears plaid pajama pants and shuts the door.

I turn off the light and let my head hit the pillow. I close my eyes, and lay as still as a mummy. I listen as Mark's footsteps head downstairs, and my body relaxes as if I've just completed a marathon.

Okay, what should I do? I mean, I wouldn't ever leave my son, but I also know how to handle him. Mark is at work all day and doesn't get time to learn the ways-of-the-toddler. And, honestly, he's not the most patient person.

How would my Mom handle this? My parents are logical. They sit down every night with a glass of wine, extra sharp Wisconsin cheddar, and the nine o'clock news. They don't get overwhelmed by emotion. My mom says, "there's nothing you can't figure out if you logically talk it over," and they've never had a fight. Yes, you heard that right. I can't remember one time my parents disagreed about something; at least, disagreed enough to yell at each other.

So, my Mom looks at the facts and doesn't get angry. Or sad. Like any good German-American. Crying is for funerals, and anger is for people who aren't as logical, or smart, as us. Yeah, my family is a little bit inflated in the ego column. In general, I talk to my Mom about Mark's little annoyances. The little things I try to indirectly tell him to do, like replace the long light bulbs in the garage or install shelves in the toy room. She gets my stay-at-home-mom frustration. However, I don't talk to her when Mark yells. I know she doesn't have experience dealing with the anger.

I lay still and quiet long enough that Mark reenters the room and climbs in bed next to me. I regulate my breathing so it sounds like I'm asleep. Soon, Mark is sound asleep. His snores the only sound in the house. I won't talk to him until I'm ready to have a logical discussion. For now, he can just deal with my silence. I fall asleep soon after.

Two Dos

Just like breathing
I pick up home
after you, me,
two children, living.
Constant beating,
metronome tone.

Just like Mother,
apron: buttoned
Mommyhood-tight,
tick, and another
load of diapers
done. When's dinner?

Ten-thousand tocks.
Proud of my clean
drawers, especially
children who paint on
the walls. God made
us to laugh, right?

The beats, now,
skipping and tripping,
tempo increasing,
frustration leaking.
Look, Dad's been demoted.
I'm now a mom
of...three?

CHAPTER 3
Spanx

LATER THAT WEEK at 6:34am, the studio lights blaze hot. I look down and smooth my green leopard print clingy dress. I try not to touch my hair, probably the first time it's been done since my daughter was born. I try not to move. My hands are freezer-cold and it feels like a sandbag is anchored to my arm. Whew, that's only my daughter. For a minute there, I thought I was having a heart attack.

My little sprite starts jumping up and down, "What's that, Mommy?"

I crouch down in my boots with the four-inch heels, a move as risky as taking a piece from a dwindling Jenga tower. I hold Barbie's arms, firmly and gently, and take out my best librarian voice.

"Sweetheart, we are in a place where they make shows that people watch on their TVs. It's called a TV-studio." I turn and point to the TV-camera with the on-air light. "That's one of their recorders. We need to be quiet," I say, putting my index finger to my lips.

Barbie's eyes go wide as she looks at the light, "What's that light, Mommy?"

Okay, it's time to break out the bribe.

"Barbie, we both need to be quiet, or we won't get donuts," I say, looking at her directly.

Quiet.

Success!

I look down at my daughter, her headful of blonde curls a triumph. Her slate-blue sprite eyes are staring up at me. Was that hour of screaming that accompanied the hair curling, which also made me think about drinking at 5am, really worth it? The blue and cream floral princess dress highlights her twinkling eyes better than any Precious Moments' figurine. She looks like a cherub or a vampire child. Either way, adorable.

I'm pulled out of my reverie by my friend's voice. It is my turn to go on our local CBS morning show for my friend's boutique. I look up, make eye-contact with my friend, and firmly grab Barbie's hand. I do a quick roll of the shoulders, feel the comforting dig of the Spanx spandex corset cut into my ribcage, and walk on air. Well, not ON air, but you know what I mean.

My main worry is not tripping. Grace is not one of my strong suits. Yeah, I've walked headfirst into poles in between doors before, and I quit ballet at age seven before they could fire me. I don't think they make pointe shoes double-wide, anyway. Let's just say, with my barely-over-five-foot frame, my parents didn't ever encourage me to go into modeling.

My friend needed some "regular moms" to showcase her local boutique. Why not? But, ugh, why? My stomach reminds me that I need a bathroom whenever I pass a certain "nervous" threshold.

The next minute is a blur. The only thing that could have been better was Barbie not fluttering around the studio like a butterfly. At least viewers got a realistic view of her dress as it would be worn by a toddler.

Afterwards, as I lay the Spanx on my bed, I feel an odd kinship with it.

I am Housewife, Midnight Volunteer, Daughter, Coffee-drinker, Survivor of Mommy-hood. I AM the Spanx. I hold our lives together. I smooth over all the rough edges. The disappointments. The vomit on the wall at 2am. The times when my husband has to work late. Or golf. I sit on the floor at Meijer next to the fish tanks with two melted-down babies, a bottle, and an open Cheerios box while our ice cream drips from the cart. I hold everything in and make it better. No tears, no shouts. A life lived smoothly, even if it makes it hard to breathe.

CHAPTER 4

Fine, just fine

THE NEXT COUPLE OF WEEKS I make sure the kids are clean and pre-fed. What does pre-fed mean? Well, I feed Jonathan and Barbie a quarter of their food before dinner, so they aren't cranky at the table. Then Mark's probability of being cranky at the dinner table goes down too, and the result is I get a warm meal. Mommy pro-tip right there, probably my only one, so enjoy it.

Dinner is on the table at five. It's not like I'm *pretending* nothing happened, but I *also* want to live in a peaceful household. So the next Saturday morning I casually say to him while handing him his morning coffee, "Hey, why don't you hang out with the guys and watch football this weekend? You haven't done that in a while, and you've been working a lot!"

The next week I iron all of Mark's khakis and polos. While heading out to go get some bread and milk one night after dinner, I peek in the toy room to say goodbye and notice he is on the phone with his work. Yes, on the phone during his kid time. Words escape my mouth before I can reel them back in.

"*Sure* you can manage the kids while I run to County Market? You're not gonna lose them, right?"

Mark gives me the death stare and continues his phone call. Well, *now* I feel better, now I feel like that incident was no big deal. Things smoothed over.

However, a couple of times during those weeks I feel that dark, looming presence in the corner of my eye. It takes a concerted effort of kitchen drawer re-organizing to forget about it . . .

CHAPTER 5
Ragu

BEING A MOM-OF-TODDLERS reminds me of the Mothers and More meal train that I signed up for before my daughter was born. Mothers and More is a local moms group. I don't know exactly what they do, I joined because I heard about the free food. I mean, the big benefit to this group is that if you have a new baby, other moms bring you dinner. Nice, right?

One night, the week after Barbie came home, a mom from the meal train knocked on our side door. It was pouring outside, that cold late-fall rain that makes even your heart cold. I opened the door, and a hooded mom was huddled under the porch roof. She thrust two soggy one-gallon Ziplock bags at me. In the alley was her minivan. Even at fifty feet I could hear wailing. This woman needs me to bring her a meal, I thought. I looked down. One bag with noodles, the other Ragu.

"Thanks so much," I said, but she didn't even look up. She tightened her raincoat hood, then turned to leave.

Finally, she mumbled, "I'm sorry. We're all sick. Congratulations on your baby."

That's how I feel a lot. Like I'm supposed to be some kind of fancy Quiche Lorraine, and instead I'm a Ziploc bag of cold spaghetti.

Speaking of cold bags of soggy noodles, that reminds me of something. My sex life. No, no, Mark has all the proper operating equipment. But I just don't like sex. I am not sure if I have the correct equipment for *enjoyment* with another human. It's kinda like a chore. Yes, I've written it on my to-do list before, it's that bad. And, not to beat a wet noodle, I will say that my daughter had exactly *one* chance to be in this world, and she took it. So I know she's gonna be President or something climate-consequential, and I'm definitely going to teach her how to boil potatoes before she leaves for college, so she'll be way ahead of me.

I have thought that I could be asexual or something. No man I encounter really makes me want to DO anything physical, so mostly what Mark and I do is hold hands. Our relationship reminds me of the Minnie and Mickey ornament we got at Disney World on our honeymoon. He's safe and comfortable and fun, and a great provider, so how can I complain? I feel pretty lucky.

How lucky was I that we found each other in the last year in college? He and I both went on a trip to a national civil engineering convention in Boston. He got really sick, like he wasn't even enjoying his beer at the Cheers bar. Luckily I had my grandma's 1940's powder-blue toiletry suitcase full of medicine, and Mark was able to enjoy the last day of our trip. Our relationship was born out of some Heidi-tender-loving-care.

Yep, I don't like to travel without my ten pounds of NyQuil, bandages, rubbing alcohol and Sudafed. You get the picture. You just never know who is going to get a laceration, and how far away the nearest Walgreens will be, even if you are in Boston.

But honestly, when Mark and I got married, I didn't know how hurtful he could be. Not, like, he's gonna beat me kinda hurt. But suddenly it's like there's red hot chili pepper sprinkled all over my life that makes my food inedible. Maybe I should have really noticed when he talked about how spicy his dad was growing up. So, I don't know how to fix him, other than smoothing it over.

CHAPTER 6

Rewind to the alley

BEFORE WE REALLY get into the weeds, I need to let you know three important things. Two things about me, and one very important someone. Here is the first.

Eighteen months prior to now, it is springtime. Springtime in the Midwest, which means the tulips, trees, bushes, and allergies in full bloom. After a nebulizer treatment for Barbie's allergy-asthma, and doses of allergy meds for the three of us, we are ready to enjoy the great outdoors.

Ninety minutes later, I find myself in the middle of an alley, the alley that runs alongside the Farmhouse. My shoulders aching and burning with every step. I am almost home, but I have to stop because Jonathan and Barbie are getting too heavy to pull. I parallel park the red radio flyer wagon, with both of them in it, on the side of the uneven gravel alleyway. The Farmhouse is about 50 yards up. I blow my nose with the last remaining tissue, and let my arms dangle like a rag-doll.

"Mommy, are you okay?" asked Jonathan.

I put my arms on my shins and look up to a son with a furrowed brow.

"Yes sweetheart. Mommy just needs a break from pulling you and your sister, I still have the sniffles." I sneeze.

"Bwess Mommy!" says Barbie, her chubby hands together in prayer.

I laugh and smile, "Thanks, sweetie."

I kneel down in the alley next to their radio flyer wagon and look at them. Barbie is all in pink, including a baseball hat protecting her head of baby fine white hair. Her wide, proud smile over clutching her prized possession, Mommy's empty coffee cup. Her nose, red from sniffles, makes her picture-perfect. Her backdrop is a bush in full bloom with a million tiny bright yellow flowers. I pull out my camera and take her picture. This will look great in their monthly slideshow for the grandparents. I already know the caption, *Blooming Barbie*.

Jonathan hops out of the wagon, wipes his nose, and declares, "I will pull Barbie, Mommy!"

A cascade of relief flows down my spine.

"Thanks, Jonathan, that would be great."

He pushes his California-blonde locks out of his face, his chubby hands grab the handle, and his face beams with pride. They forge home, uphill. Well, Midwestern uphill. His sister claps and cheers him on while I bring up the rear like an old lady in need of a cane. And the only thing I think is how come I don't feel excited about this. How come everything feels like I'm taking pictures for a slideshow that I'm never in.

CHAPTER 7
Rewind to the playground

SOON AFTER THE ALLEY comes the second important thing. The *someone*.

A couple weeks later, I am driving Miss Daisy. A cloudy, warm afternoon, one of those first days where you actually think about not wearing any coat. Jonathan and Barbie are buckled into the back seat in complementary blue and pink fleece coats. Yeah, I'm not much of a risk taker. I look into the rearview mirror, "who's ready to go to the park?"

Squeals of delight answer me from the back seat. Outside is like a *whole new world* to this stay-at-home-mom after winter. Yes, a whole new world, just like in *Aladdin*. A happy dance emanates from my heart.

"Aww, yeah, aww yeah! And who's gonna go on the big boy swing all by himself?"

I look in the side-view mirror and catch a smile, "Me!" Jonathan triumphantly declares.

A swell washes over me, "I am so proud of you, Jonathan! Do you know, you guys were the best little people this morning, do you know that? You got some energy from a nap. I took a long shower and drank my coffee H-O-T. That spells hot! AND we won't have to worry about any missing mittens, because today is April. Do you know what that means?"

Silence.

Honestly, I didn't think my son would get that, but it was worth a try.

"It's getting warmer and we can play outside more!" I continue. More cheers erupt from the back seat. I put Miss Daisy in reverse, turn on "Buzz Buzz" from Laurie Berkner, and we start our two-minute drive.

We arrive at a park with strategically placed trees and picnic shelters, tennis courts. There's a little jungle gym next to the place where the merry-go-round used to be. Why were those so dangerous again? Anyway, I like this park because there are two rows of long swings, the good kind with solid metal chains. I heft Jonathan into a regular swing and place my sprite-of-a-Barbie in a baby swing. I look at them in wonder.

When will they get real hair? Barbie is almost bald. The whisper of hair she does have reminds me of a David-Bowie mullet. Jonathan is just long-ish all over. A true California blonde. I used to have their platinum blond until I gave birth, now it's just a sandy-dishwater-blonde. Mom-blonde. Which fits, I guess, but don't have to be happy about it. At least I don't have any chin hair.

I start pushing my daughter on the baby swing, and my son abandons his. Well, that didn't last long.

Seems he has spied a new little friend, about the same age, same size. Long, brown, wavy hair in two ponytails rising and falling behind her like dolphins jumping as she skips. He helps her on the slide. Soon they are hand-in-hand laughing and playing on the mulched playground. I start chatting with Barbie.

"Oh my gosh, Barbie! Look at that. Your brother is such a sweet little guy!" I declare.

"Yes, your son is a consummate gentleman," a smooth voice answers.

Surprised, I miss the next push of Barbie on her swing and look to my side. A few swings down stands another mom, or babysitter, maybe? She's like a life-size model of an **actual** Barbie doll with a perfect platinum blonde bob. Nonchalantly pushing a petite brown-haired baby on the baby swing. Man, it feels weird to talk to other adults during the day. I need to get out more.

"Oh, thanks! Is he with...your daughter?" I say.

I think that was a quick recovery. I look down to make sure I don't have too many stains on my sweatshirt and tighten my ponytail. Honestly, I don't think that woman actually birthed those kids. She looks like some kind of model.

"Yep, she's mine," she answers. "Her name is Lynette. This little man . . . " She catches the baby boy around the middle and gives him a kiss on the cheek . . ." is Matt. And I'm Mary."

"Hi, I'm Heidi. Nice to meet you! Come here often?"

"Sometimes. You?"

"Only when I can overcome the stay-at-home-mom gravitational pull."

We both laugh.

And just like that Mary and I start texting and play-dating. Our kids were just made to be friends. Four kids under the age of five who get along **all the time** is about as rare as oceanfront property in Arizona.

What's even more coincidental is that her marriage isn't perfect either. I'll just say sometimes her hubby is not at home **or** being a doctor at the hospital, but instead breaking marriage vows, if you know what I mean.

To top that, talking with Mary feels like my Winnie-the-Pooh blankie when I was young. I used to put it over my eyes if I had a bad dream so no others could get in.

CHAPTER 8

Thirty-two

AND here is the third important thing. A few months
later it is noon on my birthday, a hot, humid day in early
August.

Mary and I and our kids are out for a special picnic. We
are surrounded by a perfectly manicured grassy corridor,
flanked on both sides by tall concrete pillars; at the top of
each is a shiny royal blue ceramic statue of a happy dragon.
Outside of the corridor is surrounded by forest. We are
picnicking at a restored mansion with English gardens from
the early nineteenth century that's now open to the public.
Thank God for the guy who donated this. The house and
grounds are a major change from the rest of the landscape
around here, corn and soybeans. It's like stumbling into Oz
in the middle of Kansas._

Today, I picked the place where we went because
it's my birthday. Usually, I take everyone's opinions into
consideration when I plan outings to the park or make
dinner, even deciding what to wear. But not today. I feel like
God gave me this one day and I can eat and ask for whatever
I need. Today, I wanted a picnic.

Our kids, already done with their picnic lunches, are
running around and laughing in the August sunscape. We sit

enjoying the rest of the lunch Mary brought for me, which includes a fresh chicken salad with red wine vinaigrette, walnuts, and grapes, AND white wine. I lay down on the blanket with my wine, propped up by my elbow. I feel like a mom-goddess.

Mary takes a small, plain cardboard box out of her purse and puts it in front of me, with a card. "You know, you didn't have to do this," I say. I feel really spoiled. This is too much. Mary has a look on her face, like she's hiding a secret.

"C'mon! You only turn thirty-two once," she says.

I close my eyes after a bite of mixed greens and goat cheese.

"Mmmm. This is so good. And isn't it so nice that the kids all like each other?"

Mary looks at the kids, then back to me.

"Hey! You haven't got all day before they come back. Open the gift!"

I pull open the lightly-taped box and pull out a plainly wrapped purple plastic kitchen gadget. It's cylindrical, about six inches, and smooth. Is this for mixing? Is Mary a Pampered Chef rep too? Damn, this woman is the whole package. I continue to investigate.

"Is this like a bottle warmer or something?"

I look further and spy some batteries in the bottom of the box.

"Oh! It's an immersion blender for healthy shakes!"

Mary almost spits out her wine. Well, that wasn't it. Mary pats my shoulder, and with a mother-knows-best voice and says,

"Heidi, this is a *vibrator*."

I sit up, turn completely away from the kids, and hold it at arm's length. I feel my ears turn sunburn-hot.

"Whoa," I say.

Mary laughs, "Haven't you ever seen one?"

"Um, no?"

I look at the little purple gadget. How does vibration even help us ladies? It's so small... Mary interrupts my thinking and raises her glass.

"Well, here's to you being a self-sufficient woman, momma!"

A smile wipes out my thought stream, I raise my glass and nod my head. Looking at the little purple gadget.

"I have no idea what I'm gonna do with you, but all my teddy bears get a name, so you do too. Welcome to the family, Juliet!"

CHAPTER 9

On the menu every night

NOW THAT YOU KNOW the three important things, let's get back to the present.

It's dinner time. I buckle Barbie into her travel high chair, a kind of chair that grips onto the side of the kitchen table with rubber feet. Jonathan, fourteen months her senior, climbs and buckles himself into his booster chair. Such a self-sufficient little man.

Today I gave myself a break with dinner. I made mashed potatoes and microwave carrots. Mark got to help make dinner after work for the first time in since I can remember, grilled chicken, which was great because at least the chicken was hot off the grill. I had to reheat the potatoes and carrots and feed some to the kids; he was late and didn't bother telling me. I'm not happy. I stand between the kids and start hacking apart the chicken breast for them.

"So, you were late today. How come you didn't tell me?"

Yes, I'm opening up a can of worms.

Mark brushes off my comment like a fleck of dandruff off his shoulder.

"I told you I would be late sometime this week."

What am I, a mind reader? He gives no apologies, ever. Why do I even try? My stomach reminds me I can't win and it's also empty, so I might as well smooth things over. I finish cutting up the kids' chicken, take a deep breath, and sit down.

"So, how was work?" I ask. I can tell Mark likes the new line of conversation.

"Good! Started to work on a proposal, then me and a couple of guys went to lunch."

Sounds like Mark had plenty of time to not be late for dinner. I look down and focus on my food.

"Mhm. nice. Where did you go?" I ask in between bites.

"So we went to . . ." Mark starts.

"I got to go potty," Jonathan chimes in.

Oh no, here goes. At least I can get in a few shovelfuls before...

"Hey buddy, that's not polite to interrupt the adults." Mark states. His words are final. The table is silent. Jonathan unbuckles his seat and climbs down, his eyes and mouth cautious.

"I'm sorry, Daddy. I gotta go potty."

"You gonna be a big boy and go all by yourself?" Mark asks. His countenance brightens.

Jonathan's wide smile returns, "Yeah!"

Mark picks up his fork and knife and continues,

"So as I was saying, we went to TGI Friday's. It wasn't that busy."

Out of the side of my eye, I notice Jonathan isn't moving. I nod to him like I'm saying **get movin!** I look over at Mark and continue, "That sounds great. What did you eat?"

A tug on my arm almost pulls the fork out of my hand.

"Can you come, Mommy?" my son asks, his Bambie-hazel eyes pleading with me. Before I can respond Mark does.

"Hey Buddy, can you just go by yourself? Like a big boy?"

I can tell Jonathan wants company. I join in the conversation.

"Mark, well, since you are home, why don't you go with him?"

Mark puts down his fork and knife. Jonathan's face drops. Something else is gonna drop if one of us doesn't go.

"This is my first break all day," Mark huffs. He picks his silverware back up.

"So anyway, I got a bacon cheeseburger and fries and a salad."

"Well, that sounds delightful," I say as I stand up.

I turn to Jonathan, "Okay little man, let's go. I wonder if you will get two or four M&Ms?" He grabs my hand and starts pulling me toward the potty "four!"

After dinner, bath time, book, and bed, Mark and I meet in the living room for our nightly ritual: TV. Mostly we watch reality TV like Bachelor, Amazing Race, Survivor or American Idol. I've tried but I just can't do Real Housewives or Big Brother. Those people seem to have too much time on their hands. Mark sits in his La-Z-Boy, I take the couch.

I'm distracted from the shows tonight because of our dinner conversation. A few months ago, Mark's comment and lateness from work wouldn't bother me, but now I'm annoyed. Doesn't he, at the very least, want to give his wife a break? What year is it again?

CHAPTER 10
Covered

What is with all these blankets?
Suffocating underneath,
dead air.

Is it from your lungs?
Weighty and shielded from all,
hunched in your woven cave.

Why didn't you pull them off?
My cracked hands,
bleeding from years of
Knitting,

I have made these blankets.
Well, honey, I no longer want to feel like
your maid, servant,
slave, human, asleep.

Will you even help me?
Aching to breathe,
yearning to unravel,
myself after all these covers.

CHAPTER 11

Who needs Church?

THAT SUNDAY, I find myself in my new favorite seat. I stare lovingly at the hot Styrofoam cup of weak coffee between my hands. You know, that kind of coffee where an extra quarter of a teaspoon of sugar is the difference between bliss and wincing while slowly sucking it in between your teeth? Yeah, I'm living dangerously today, like a free woman.

High, dark, vaulted ceilings and stain-glass windows offer air. A fish can really breathe in here, and then there's that old-church-building smell. You could really recruit new people to come to church if you just bottled that smell. I close my eyes and take a deep, long breath.

Today I don't have to do three mom-of-toddler chores at church. What are the chores? Well, first, I don't need to constantly check if Barbie is crawling underneath the pews. Second, I don't need to reach like a Weeping Angel to offer a pencil for coloring that actually has a point in the middle of the sermon. Last, and certainly not least, I won't be apologizing to everyone in our pew when one of my kids needs to go to the bathroom when we walk right in front of them.

A church friend sitting next to me knows this is my first time without the kids, squeezes my hand, and whispers, "How you doing over there?" All smiles on my end.

Six months. That's how long it took to earn this quiet. Barbie was going through her *I don't like anyone but Mommy* phase right when we joined this church so, you guessed it, I've been in the nursery. Now, as a bud feels its first rays of sun as a flower, I am free.

Honestly, I don't know if I believe in God. I just need a church to get my kids baptized in. Isn't that important? I dunno. I think so? Mark and I looked at a lot of churches around town and settled on McRibben Presbyterian.

I just really like it because everyone here is, oh, what's that word again? Casual? Nope. Feminine? Not that, either. *Feminist*. Yep! This church is all about equality, which is... what's the word? Dangerous? Kinda. Surprising? A little. *Refreshing for a church*. Yep, that's it.

The Presbyterian Pastor who confirmed me as a teenager was all about fire and brimstone and *women's place*, so our church exists in the 21st century.

Another reason I like it is that one of the pastors is GAY. I've never known any gay ladies before, with the exception of my first boss at the Girl Scout Council. But she was also bipolar and wouldn't take her meds sometimes. So, you can imagine, I never really got to know her.

But my gay Pastor is like a unicorn, intriguing and magical. I wonder if she loves her wife like husbands love their wives, and if one of them is more like a husband. Hmmm.

In any case, God, I pray that some of this Sunday lady power will have a nice effect on Mark's parenting, and thank you for this coffee. Amen.

CHAPTER 12

Fool me twice

THE EARLY JANUARY SUN shines brightly into the tall windows of our dining room in the early afternoon. Barbie, in her IKEA-took-me-six-hours-to-put-together-five-pieces-of-wood-and-three-metal-rods-toddler chair, is snacking like a happy snail on a jar of meat sticks and a pile of peas. Why do I even bother with dinner with all these snacks? I am reading *One Fish, Two Fish* to her for the seventh time today.

The kitchen door slams shut, and my son rushes over behind my chair, ducking for cover. Good grief. I put the book down. Not even stopping to say hello while putting away his coat, Mark yells, "**Go ahead, Jonathan,**" not even stopping to say hello while putting away his coat. "Tell Mommy where you wandered off to today."

My stomach sinks. I turn around and look at my little trembling boy. I thought we were over this issue. Mark pauses on his way to the kitchen and sticks his head in the room. He needs to give me an explanation, now.

"**Excuse me. What?**" I demand.

I look straight at Mark. I can see this is the bait he is looking for.

"**Well, Jonathan wouldn't come with me to get the hardware,**" he lets off steam, like fresh lava hissing as it touches the ocean. "**So I left him in the door section.**"

I feel that dark presence in the corner of my eye, and my heart starts to pound. It's getting. Closer. I push on. Why can't Mark, at least, apologize?

"So, you left him alone at Menards?" I say, turning around to unzip Jonathan's coat and hanging it on the back of my chair. I heft Jonathan on my lap and hand him and Barbie some goldfish.

"See? He's fine." Mark says, raising his arm and gesturing at the table. "A store person brought him up to the front."

So that's it, no harm, no foul? Don't they convict people who attempt unsuccessfully to kill people? Or do they say, 'Oh, you didn't kill her, so you can go home now.' This is **just like** the first time. Jonathan is more cautious than a feral cat, which lets me know it's not about him.

Mark folds his arms and his brow darkens. There's nothing else I can say that won't escalate into yelling. I get up from the table, but then words accidentally punch out of my mouth.

"This is not okay." Okay, Heidi, you said your peace. Now take it down a notch. I take a breath. "Can you please finish with Barbie?" I ask.

Oh no, I've unleashed the Kraken.

"How is this my fault? He's not being a, oh, what do you call it, a first-time-listener!" Marks voice rumbles like a thunderstorm.

How can Mark even think this is about his son? I look down and Jonathan is ducking so well he'd pass an air raid drill. I stand and pick him up. Time to get my son to a safe bunker.

"He's *three*. What do you expect?" I ask.

"For our son to obey his father!"

Ha! Even Darth Vader couldn't make his son do that. I'm done. Mark deserves nothing more from me. I carry Jonathan upstairs into his big boy room where I place him on his bed and rub his back. I stare at his dump truck comforter. What can I do now? Trying to focus on this question is like trying to take a sip from a waterfall. After a while, Jonathan turns and looks up at me, eyes shining.

"Was I a bad boy, Mommy?"

Oh, great. Now he's sad and scared. I give him a big side hug.

"No sweetheart. Not. At. All."

Twice. My husband is a degreed engineer, does he need, like, a parenting class? I mean, once my parents left my oldest, loudest, brother at a gas station in the middle of Arizona. They said that he was really nice in the car after that. But that was once. An accident.

And two summers ago, in the middle of our neighborhood garage sale Jonathan defeated a toddler lock, two baby gates, and the backdoor, to play in the back of our minivan while I breastfed Barbie. I had the whole neighborhood looking for him. I get it. These things happen.

BUT this is twice. A pattern. A trend.

Am I the fool now?

I feel that dark looming presence still with me, and I swallow a lump in my throat. Maybe Mary will know what to do.

PART TWO

THE
RED QUEEN

CHAPTER 13
A million sighs

Like the lava beneath every surface,
my Anger has no year.
No birth.
It is who I have become
because of you.

My soul's choke
my sigh has no voice.
No way.
It is only I can't say
because of you.

CHAPTER 14

Emergency Mary
Playdate #1

IT'S A FEW DAYS LATER AT LUNCHTIME, in a new mansion in a quiet cul-de-sac on the outskirts of our corn-framed snow-covered college town. Mary's house. Once inside, I am surrounded by beautiful dark wood flooring, stainless steel appliances, granite countertops, and oversized furniture. Above the mantle is her wedding picture from Hawaii. In an elegant, slim, strapless white gown, she and her tuxedoed husband are surrounded by the green and vibrant lushness. She looks so happy. Looks can be totally deceiving.

After the first ten minutes, kids' laughter bubbles from the downstairs playroom. Well, normally, that happens right away. But my little man has been a bit clingy since the Menards incident. I can't blame him. After showing him where I was going to sit on the couch and walking him downstairs, for the second time, he stayed.

At the top of the stairs, Mary hands me some peace of mind, a crisp glass of Riesling. I melt into her soft taupe couch. She places another prize in front of me, my very own Panera salad. Mary and I are like fairy friend-mothers to each other. My heart is happy.

When you're used to leftover sticky mac and cheese, and soggy chicken nuggets, a salad and a glass of wine is like a miracle in the middle of the daily mom-slog. Especially today. I glance up at the picture, "So, is your husband ever home?"

Mary rolls her eyes and frowns. I can tell this was not the question she is hoping for. "Well, as a cardiologist, he works shifts," she answers. "He has to sleep at the hospital a lot. And he knows I am still not happy with him because of his continuing behavior." She puts her hand on my leg. "So, lady, what's this I hear about another child abandonment?"

"Yep, I dunno what to do now. Any ideas?"

"You could always try the counseling route," Mary says. Oh yeah, why didn't I think of that?

"That sounds like a possibility. But..." I hesitate.

Mary's eyes widen like a wildebeest. She catches her breath and leans in closer.

"Oh my God, Heidi, do you feel Mark's going to hit you? or the kids?"

I shake my head in disagreement. Well, at least that's something positive.

"No, no. Not at all. But something *worse* is going to happen."

Yeah, I'm talking about you, creepy looming darkness in the corner of my eye.

A huge sigh comes out of Mary's mouth, and she leans back into the couch.

"Well, thank god! And, Heidi, I think all this seriousness is getting to you. Maybe you

need a little a girl's-night-out with my friends," she suggests. I couldn't agree more.

Lighthouse

The light,
your light,
a beacon of hope
in my stormy sea.
This lost soul,
navigating to refuge
because of you,
even if that means
searing high heels,
bad Janet Jackson karaoke, and
buckling in drunk
in your toddler seat
for a safe ride home.
Cannot wait
for the next ride.

CHAPTER 16

We interrupt your regularly scheduled programming to bring you: My Thumb

MY RIGHT THUMB HURTS. Like the side part of the thumb that goes up the arm. Now, there are many classifications of *this hurts* between me and my kiddoes. Let me explain.

Bumper. This acknowledgment of an inflicted wound comes immediately after any such incident, including falling down while walking, hitting one's head on a door knob, brushing against something unexpected, like a plant, or being pushed over while racing to the coveted snack seat in the Church nursery. While no physical sign or remnant of injury exists, the truth must be heard as quickly as possible. Mommy lap time is discouraged. However, there will certainly be hugs with a soothing pat on the back.

Boo boo. Like a *bumper,* a *boo boo* has no sign of redness or marking in the area, but the hurt must be acknowledged with a kiss, Mommy lap time for five minutes, and a cold wash rag application for an equal amount of time.

Ouchie. There is, upon use of a tool such as a magnifying glass or flashlight, a faint sign of redness, possibly a *cut*.

However, we do not use that term in our household. It's too scary. Much fanfare accompanies the *ouchie*. First, we have a full thirty-minute Mommy-lap session with a favorite *Mickey Mouse Clubhouse* episode. Next comes a gentle cleansing with salve application and, finally, is the parade over to the band-aid box to contemplate if there will be a *Thomas the Tank Engine* or *Backyardigans* band-aid.

Doozie. The real words that describe this kind of injury are cuss words, often aimed at the other parent. A trip to the *special doctor*, also known as the Emergency Room, is actively in play. Examples include skin sliced away on the knee that reveals bone and skin bubbling up from a third-degree sunburn. While much needs to be done amidst tears, Mommy stays calm, carries her child around for the next two days, and reapplies medicine every half hour. With a *Doozie*, Mom does not get any sleep, as her mom-dar is up at full volume.

My thumb is a *Doozie.* Whenever it moves, spikes of pain travel up my arm, like red hot surgery needles piercing, melting, soldering me from thumb to elbow, over and over. It's called Mommy-Thumb. Not technically, of course. I have gotten two cortisone shots for it already, but it's getting worse. I think it's probably because I didn't use those baby carriers a lot when the kids were little. Mostly, I carry my close-to-Irish-twins around with my bare hands.

Now, I am left-handed. So you might think, "How come the *right* thumb has the issue?" Let me tell you what this left-handed Mommy does with her *right* hand. First, I open cans and boxes, otherwise known as *dinner*. Second, I lift the heavy grocery bags and the heavier toddler, but not at the same time, of course. So yeah, my right arm is the muscles.

I can't live like this.

My back tightens as I dial the phone. I wince from a breeze brushing across my thumb. My mom will know what to do.

"Hi Mom, good morning! How are you?"

Pause

"Oh, we're all good over here. How's Dad?"

Why can't I just ask for help?

Maybe because Mom never needed help. She is a self-sufficient German-American. She got five hours of sleep a night, made every meal, and sewed everyone's clothes, including the coveted Batman and Robin Halloween costumes, *and* got her Master's in Teaching. I'm not doing any of that. Just two toddlers. And I still need help. #Momfail.

My stomach wrenches. I can't ask. I am failing at all of this. I listen for a few more minutes, we talk about dinner plans and their next visit. I hang up, defeated.

I drag my feet to the bathroom, shut the door, and cry. Why do I have to cry? It's just a stupid thumb. I hate crying. It makes me feel worse.

In bed that night, I stare at the ceiling and contemplate different ways to cut my thumb off. Do I have a sharp enough knife? What about that circular saw I inherited from my Great Uncle Ronald? That's never even been used, and it still has the 1954 instruction manual. I squeeze my eyes shut. I don't know if I have the stomach to handle that...I need a drastic change. I need to cross the line.

I gently tap Mark on the shoulder, "Hey Mark? You awake?"

"No, but I am now." He rolls over to face me, "What's up?"

It's time to tell him.

"I think my thumb needs surgery."

CHAPTER 17
Let's get physical

THREE WEEKS, ONE SURGERY, and visits from my and Mark's mom that include homemade dinners I didn't have to cook . . .

I walk into a square wide-open room, with what looks like a giant tumbling mat in the center. Rows of resistance machines, racks of giant colorful balls and rubber straps line the room. On one wall, there are several what-look-to-be a cross between a doctor's exam table and a massage table. One chair is set on either side of an empty one.

"Okay, Heidi. Have a seat," offers Roy.

So this is my physical therapist? This skinny, fifty-something, ultra-tan man looks like he spends more time on a tanning bed than at work. My heart starts to pound, a dull ache spreads across my back. Oh God, is this gonna hurt worse? Roy sits across the table from me. It's like he just read my mind.

"Okay, Heidi. This might feel uncomfortable."

He cradles my arm in one of his and rolls up my sleeve. His hands feel rough against mine, but in a way that makes me feel every single touch. He pushes his fingers, firm and hard, up my forearm, to bring heat and blood to the area. To heal. I close my eyes. Every molecule of my being is focused on his touch. I feel 30. Vibrant. Blooming. Cared for.

"Hey, Heidi?" a deep voice knocks on my mind. I jolt myself back to the room. My face grows hot from embarrassment.

"Oh, yeah. I'm here. I'm here," I say.

"Good. I hope that didn't hurt too much. We're all done today." He hands me a paper that looks like a sign language worksheet. "Here are the exercises to do at home. Please call me if you have questions. Remember to schedule your sessions twice a week for the next six weeks."

Fuck yeah, I will.

"Thanks, this was great. You're really good at this therapy thing." I blurt out while walking away, staring at the sheet.

I get to the front desk. My whole body is heated and my brain feels fuzzy. I stop at the water fountain to recalibrate. Ugh, why did I bring the diaper bag?

I take out my normally-on-my-wall calendar that has every checkup, playdate, and visit from my parents marked down for the year. Oh crap. Did I forget the sticky notes with my neighbor's availability to watch the kids during therapy? I rifle through the diaper bag. It's so dark down there.

Finally something sticks to my hand. Whew. They seem to have attracted a wide assortment of goldfish crumbs. I brush off the crumbs. My neighbors are the best.

Walking out of the building, clutching my therapy schedule, I look up to a hopeful blue sky. Roy's therapy felt like the kindest, most selfless thing anyone's ever done for me. Like I'm not taking the picture for the slideshow any more. Like I'm IN the picture.

As I slide into Miss Daisy, I start deflating. Back to reality. Every drop of my heat evaporates. Tears gather in the corners of my eyes. Why do I always have to ruin everything by crying? A large weight grows in my chest. I need a plan to fix my current situation. How about a plan my mom would be proud of? Something indirect, yet effective.

CHAPTER 18
I, first, try this

OVER THE NEXT TWO WEEKS I am like a Mother Hen. Always pecking around, following Mark and the kids to the store, to the backyard swing set, to the car. The hours, minutes, seconds drag on. I can't keep this up forever. I'm not made to be a Mother Hen.

Plus, Mother Hen-ning makes Mark, well, cranky. "What's your problem?" and "What are you doing?" are his new favorite questions, aimed right at yours truly.

CHAPTER 19
Not a charm

AS THE DAYS WEAR ON, I know I need a break or I'm gonna lose it. I ask Mark if he can take the kids in the backyard to play, then to grab some takeout. A short, calculated break.

I take complete advantage of their absence. I sweep and mop like a sprinter. I shower like a goddess, and I eat half of a leftover cheeseburger with an extra-large portion of Doritos like a starving man. I melt into my La-Z-Boy with a fresh cup of coffee.

God, I love that sweet-sweet no-kid quiet. If there was a candle scent for a *quiet house with no kids*, I could make a killing. I slide open the keyboard on my phone and get ready to text Mary. I exhale a contented sigh.

The kitchen door opens and slams shut. Two matching fleecy-coated toddlers run and jump on my lap. I move my coffee just in time before another matching tracksuit bites the dust. I do have a pretty great gig here.

"What little sweethearts you are!" I say, with a big hug. "Thanks for taking them, I needed that!" I add, looking up at Mark.

"No Problem," he replies. "So, there was an incident."

"Oh? What's up? Did they super-size your churros by mistake?"

I look. Nope, nobody is carrying leftovers. My heart is hopeful. Mark shifts his feet back and forth.

"Well, no. So, I took Barbie to the potty during lunch . . ."

I squeeze my little pink sweetheart.

". . . and when we got back," Mark continues, looking down, "Jonathan was gone."

My heart deflates all at once, like a squeaky balloon. Is this really happening again? Mark pauses and sets his jaw, then raises the volume.

"He just got worried and just left Taco Bell. He wasn't that far away. No big deal."

Jesus. Three times in six months. This is a pattern. What is wrong with him? I move the kids off my lap. I'm pissed. He can't abandon my kids anymore. Doesn't he know that all the stuff I do around the house is for him and the kids? *It's all I do. It's why I exist.* And it looks like he's just trying to lose his son all the time. Why?

Maybe if I make it about *us*, it will also help *him*. I hold my arms up as if I give up. "So, I don't know what to say. I'm frustrated with us. Would you be willing to talk it out with me with one of our Pastors. Maybe?"

Mark eyes me sideways, like someone's out to get him. Then, his face relaxes, he makes a pointing gesture between he and I.

"Sure, if you think that will help this."

CHAPTER 20

Pastoral Counseling

THE NEXT WEEK, Mark and I walk into McRibben's Church. Pastor Kevin, the co-pastor, comes out of a side door of the fellowship hall to greet us. This jolly man's crooked-toothed smile can light up a room. His arms open wide for a big Santa hug, which I melt into. I'm totally the hugger in the family. Finally, I'll get to tell Mark how it's not okay what he did and he needs to change. Big girl panties, check. I got this.

Pastor Kevin's office is unexpected. Small. Walls of overloaded bookcases like sentries. His desk is covered by a pile of papers like a churning sea. Balanced atop, the remnants of his last few meals. Hardees and Chipotle. Mark and I each pick up a pile of papers so we can sit.

"Thanks so much for coming." Kevin starts. "Let us all join hands and pray."

While Mark and I are normally like Mickey and Minnie, things have been growing more distant between us. I hold his sweaty hand, but I feel it is like some poison I could absorb. Come to think of it, I can't even remember the last time we hugged that was not a going-to-work or coming-home-from-work ritual. Come to think of it, our hugs are now more like waltz hugs than my regular melt-into-my-body hugs.

Kevin interrupts my thoughts, bows his head, and begins.

"Dear God. Thank you for this time with Heidi and Mark today. Let your light of awareness and bountiful love shine down on them as they reveal and heal what is in their hearts and minds today. Amen."

"Amen" Mark and I follow.

We release hands, and I look up at Kevin. Okay, here goes nothing. But before I can speak, Kevin continues, "First, you each are going to turn towards each other and say two nice things about each other."

God, really? Is this what fixes people and marriages? Patting egos? Mark jumps right in.

"Okay, I'll go first. Heidi, I appreciate how well you take care of the kids. And you do a really nice job on all of my work clothes. Ironing, I mean."

Kevin's face lights up. "Great job, Mark. Heidi?"

"Mark, you are a great provider for our family," I say, "And I appreciate how you make dinner sometimes. Like spaghetti and grilled chicken."

"Great, Heidi!" Kevin says, looking at us like a proud parent. "Now, why did I have you start that way? Well, it's been proven that to have a good, healthy relationship, you need eight positive interactions for every one that is challenging."

Wow. Our interactions are probably about eight to one. The other way.

Thirty minutes later we walk out of the office in different directions, him back to work and me to home. Yeah, I didn't say anything. Maybe it's my German-American-ness, or it's because his behavior is so frustrating. Maybe it's me.

are you there, God?

Did you say something?
Well, that took a while. Decades, even.
So I can stop running on my wheel
whenever I want
and the world will not stop?
Are you SURE?
Isn't the power grid hooked up to my wheel?
Sounds too risky.
You know, I ask you questions.
And the vast majority
of the time
I am fairly certain
you are not listening.
Or even around.
There are glimmers
when I feel You;
a hand on my back,
warmth on my face.
So I get up the courage
to ask one more time.
If I am broken.

If I can be fixed
If I am supposed to just keep running
on this wheel
for everyone else.

CHAPTER 22

Around and around we go

AFTER TWO SESSIONS, I am losing confidence in Kevin and his *pat on the back* methods. I mean, I trust him, but I don't think Mark does. Probably because I go to church more often. But I picked the dude pastor for pastoral counseling so Mark would be comfortable, so he didn't think us ladies were ganging up on him.

I waltz-hug Mark when I see him enter the Church. We walk into the small office around lunch time. The creaking of Kevin's Medieval-style door and the clicking of Mark's dress shoes against the concrete floor are the only sounds. Kevin's small windows are cranked open, and a chilly spring breeze envelops me. I zip up my light pink velour tracksuit to the top. At least it doesn't smell like nachos.

After our hug, prayer, and obligatory rounds of compliments, he hands us pieces of paper that look like a blank color wheel. Thank God it's something different.

"This is a Dialog Wheel," Kevin begins. "It's a way to talk out how you feel so you can avoid saying things that your spouse might view as attacks. It's called *I statements*."

I look down at the paper. I notice my cold hands clenching it, wrinkling it on the sides. So, I have to go through all of these *I statements* to get out whatever I'm feeling? I don't even know what I'm feeling other than mad. Maybe I should stick with the compliments. My stomach drops. It has hit its nervous threshold.

"Excuse me, I have to use the ladies room. Sorry."

I place the paper down on my chair, exit, and sloth-walk to the bathroom. I don't want to say any of these things to Mark. I feel, like, it's too dangerous or something. In the bathroom, I make a bargain with myself. If I go back in, I will skip rotating the kids toys this month. I almost skip back to Kevin's office.

"Sorry about that, I'm ready to go," I say.

"Okay, we are going to start with an easy one," Kevin starts. "Think of one thing that is a little annoying about your spouse and go around the wheel. An example could be if they leave keys in the door."

Oh, that seems safe. I can do this. Mark takes work calls during his kid time. Drives me nuts. Fifteen minutes later, you guessed it, I totally earned that free time. Mark is super annoyed about the phone call convo, though. Why can't anything with him be easy? Maybe Mary will know what to do.

CHAPTER 23

Emergency Mary Playdate #2

TWO DAYS LATER, I get ready. I shower, shave, makeup, curl, and spray on the finishing touch, Sweet Pea body spray. Then I don my best pajamas, a pale pink satin pinstripe pajama pants set. Matching undies, of course. I am ready for Mary. Just thinking about her makes me happy.

Mark is out of town for his week for his work. Yes, it happens about once a month. The great news is that my parents came to help with the kids. God, I love my parents; they are like grandparent-minute-men.

My parents are settled into their nine o'clock-WGN-news-with-cheese-and-beer regime. I tell them not to wait up for me. My mom eyes my pajamas with one eyebrow as high as a skyscraper. I chuckle to myself, I don't think she's ever left the house in pajamas.

Ten minutes later, I am met at the door by my statuesque bestie.

"Hey sexy lady, you want the usual?" says Mary with twinkling eyes. Well, at least someone's in a Mommy-mayhem mood, which usually means drinking one beverage and stalking people on Facebook. I know, so scandalous.

I smile and answer, "I will absolutely take a Stella."

Mary glides into the kitchen and I follow in her draft.

"Give me the lowdown, how's counseling? Is it working?" she asks, opening my beer.

Man, this woman cuts right to the deep stuff right away. No fluff. A heaviness presses on me, like a cloud just ruined my sunny day.

"Well, Mark is the same, if that's what you mean. I feel like I can talk more about how I am pissed, but I have this feeling like it doesn't matter. Because Mark is just, well, Mark. And he's gonna keep leaving Jonathan. And one time, Jonathan might not come back."

I put my beer down on the counter, and think that a life without Jonathan would be like a life without sun. Mary puts her arm around my shoulders.

"Maybe it's time to start thinking about the D word, Heidi. Documentation. My husband has been using pay phones to coordinate all sorts of acts that I am documenting. You know, you should be doing that, too. Just in case things get bad."

"Yeah, that sounds pretty logical . . ." I say.

We start walking to the bedroom.

"And what about money?" Mary continues, "Can you start saving a little back?"

Oh wow, I didn't think about that.

"Um, well, let me think. We have a few months of Mark's salary in savings. I don't think, if it ever gets to the point of *actually* ending things, there will be a money issue."

Mary stops, turns around and looks me up and down.

"Oh honey, I don't know if you know this. But he's gonna get a lot angrier if you end things. He is comfortable

83

with his American Dream right now. And all that anger is gonna take moola, woman."

A sun peeks out from the clouds around my heart.

"Oh, yeah, like a job. Good idea, Mary! At least that will give me options. No matter what." She puts her hand on my forearm and leans over, the twinkle coming back to her eyes.

"Exactly! And you know what? I think it's time to talk about you. How is physical therapy going with Mr. Roy?"

PART THREE

EAT ME,
DRINK ME

CHAPTER 24

Spousal Dreamland

THERAPY WITH Roy is an oasis in the middle of the unending desert of my life. Roy gives me everything I need to keep going. Mary says that different people arrive in our lives to help us, like angels. While I'm not sure Roy is an angel, he gives me oxygen.

I sometimes dream about Roy. Not in a scandalous way. Like one time he gave me a fresh club sandwich with crisp bacon and a cold Diet Coke. Another, he held my hand before I tripped in a puddle. In another, he put his arm around my waist and sat next to me while I cried, while soft waves lapped on a sandy shore. Once, he gave me a Native American blanket that smelled like *everything is going to be okay*. I would totally buy that blanket.

The last couple of weeks, I started to shower and put on makeup for therapy, too. Seriously, what do I think will happen? Roy is married, loves golf, and is 20 years older than me. And, to be honest, he's not that attractive, even with all the tanning and slimness. What do I want to happen?

CHAPTER 25

perfection

My dream partner
must have weathered a few storms in life,
knows how to not take themselves seriously,
well, most of the time.
With eyes bright enough to indicate
a sense of humor and
spontaneous playfulness.
They will never let me stand still
for too long.
And will walk with me,
give me space to dig deeper
find love, God, myself,
when I ask.
Their soul, love, and trust,
I will gently work towards
in their preciousness
as if I have a nest of baby birds in hand.
And we will know
the truest blessing in life
is in sharing
deeply and fully
with each other.

CHAPTER 26
waffling

OVER THE NEXT MONTH, I get lost in my head.
Week 1: I need to have an honest talk with Mark to get him to change. I wonder how Roy would respond. If he and I were together, I mean.

Week 2: I don't want to talk with Mark. He'll just yell again during the Dialog Wheel exercise. Yes, we tried and it happened. I can't get over him leaving Jonathan. I can't forgive him. You know, Roy is kinda sexist. I *think* he's joking, but I'm never sure. He'd probably respond with something like *kids are for women to take care of*.

Week 3: Maybe I can't forgive Mark because he's never going to apologize. I bet Roy's wife kicks him out of the house to play golf because she can't stand him. Maybe that's why he's so tan!

Week 4: Maybe Mark and I need the opposite of talking. Yeah, maybe more space. Maybe a new place will offer me a new perspective. The Farmhouse is our starter house, anyway. And I bet Roy has issues I don't even know about. I'm gonna let his wife deal with that can of worms, but I'm still going to keep the Roy-of-my-dreams.

CHAPTER 27

Operation Abode

TWO SUPER-BUSY MONTHS LATER and some cancelled sessions with Kevin, I jump up and down in the doorway of an empty house in cookie-cutter suburbs of our central Illinois town. Half brick and half white siding, porch long enough to hold red, white, and blue buntings nicely on the fourth of July. Not every house is exactly the same, so that's good. I've seen that *X-Files* episode where Mulder and Scully pose as a couple in a subdivision where every house is the same; I don't need a mud monster in my life ready to eat me if I don't take out the garbage on time.

Back to the house. Yes, it's fancy, and it feels familiar, like my parents' house and Mark's parents' house had a baby. I pause in a front carpeted room and look outside. But the main difference is if you look between the houses across the street, instead of other houses, you see fields of tiny green buds. By July, it will be a sea of cornstalks.

I holler at Mark, who is somewhere else in the house, "You like it?"

"Yeah, it's big! Did you see it has a boiling water tap in the faucet? We'll never have to heat water again!"

Oh, this house is going to be a winner. "Yeah, Fancy! I love it! Do you?"

Mark emerges from the basement, laughing, "And the basement even has room for your roller skate playdates!"

He grows wide-eyed. This is probably the happiest I've seen him, in, like, forever. Yes. Yes. This will work. "Let's do it!" I proclaim, "Welcome to *The Woodridge*!"

Mark puts his hands on his hips, proud as a father goose. "Look at us! We have arrived." We come together for a waltz-hug. Better than nothing.

CHAPTER 28

Skyward

Turning into my neck of suburbia
Minivan, kids to and fro activities,
Picket-fenced life.
On this bright blue summer sky day,
windows down, all three voices singing.

I look up from the road and see
a robust, exuberant life,
stretching arms skyward
soaking in light, love,
Hope.

Feet firmly planted, nourished, grounded,
deep in Her Earth.
soaking in life, soul, strength.
My core exalted in agreement,
a beautiful tree,
a beautiful life.

CHAPTER 29

The Battle for Middle Earth begins

A MONTH LATER and a couple more cancelled Kevin sessions later, we are moved into our new house. It's a box wonderland. I can breathe in this house. Three toy rooms, an eat-in kitchen, a fenced-in backyard. It's all great, but.

Nothing's changed. All the space makes it easier to be separate, not together. It doesn't make Mark any less likely to start arguments. It doesn't make him apologize. It doesn't make me forgive him.

What Operation Abode did give us was a book. Yep, an extra bonus for all of the missed sessions with Kevin is we have a book to read. It's called *Intimate Strangers*. Maybe some knowledge will help us.

In the meantime, I have an idea that could change everything for Mark and me. It's gonna take some courage, shopping, and a conference with Mary. But I think it will work.

CHAPTER 30
The Summer of Love

THE NEXT WEEK AT MY HOUSE, our bellies are deliciously full from a surprise pizza luncheon-playdate we threw ourselves, Mary and I. Our kids are quiet in the living room with *Backyardigans* and ice cream bars.

I lead Mary upstairs, holding her hand. I see her try to open her eyes, "No peeking!"

She laughs and keeps her eyes shut until we get to my bedroom. The stately vaulted ceilings of the master bedroom frame the dark minimal furniture and cream bedding. The sage curtains make it hushed, calm. The summer afternoon light makes the room warm like the nook of a library in the sun.

"Okay, you can open your eyes," I say, letting go of Mary's hand.

Mary opens her eyes and covers her mouth, chuckling, "Oh, Heidi. That's quite the ensemble. What is it for?"

I unveil my plan and Vanna-White the lingerie pile, "Welcome to the Summer of Love."

On the bed is a rainbow array of lingerie, lace, gloves, feather boas, garters. Sailor navy and white, leopard print magenta, red, lavender. Mary shakes her head. I nod mine and continue.

"I know, it seems like a stretch. And you know I'm not a fan of sex in general. However," I raise my index finger and my eyebrows, "Now, stay with me here. What if sex made us looser, so we could actually talk to each other. Then we can air our grievances and laugh about it, like in *Seinfeld*."

We both take a long drink of our lunchtime wine.

Walking around the bed I continue, "This is the best I could manage with the move and all. There was one negligee I couldn't find. I remember at my bridal shower, my Maid of Honor labeled it as 'white and nasty' because the chest section was detachable. I must have given it to Goodwill."

Mary softens and puts her arm around my shoulders, "Honey, if sex can't fix it, you can't say you didn't try."

"Oh! that reminds me! Lynn. Lynn is the one who is trying," I exclaim.

Mary says in a whispered hush, "Is that your secret code name?"

I wink, making the Rosie-the-Riveter arm, "You betcha. I'm donating my middle name to the cause."

"Um, Mommy? Mommy what are these?" We both are startled by the quiet visitor. Jonathan has come up from downstairs, with a mouth ringed in chocolate. He's patting the fluffy pile of lingerie. I walk over to Jonathan and kneel down in between him and my bed.

"Oh goodness, Sweetheart! Where is your ice cream bar?" I ask.

Jonathan's arms go up in the air, "Oopsy, mine fell. I need a new one. Please." He smiles triumphantly, but his eyes are focused on the bed. He leans and peers around me, "What *is* on your bed, Mommy?"

Might as well be honest. I take his hand and lead him out of the room, his eyes still focused on the lingerie. "Those are Mommy's new dresses for nighttime," I say. "How about we go wipe you and get a new treat?"

CHAPTER 31
Lynn

LATER THAT WEEK, MIDSUMMER: THE PLAN COMMENCES. Our living room. Kids in bed. Mark starts. "So, Heidi, are you ready?"

I'm cold. But I put my hand on my hip. "I **told** you, my name is Lynn."

Mark nods.

"Alrighty, **Lynn**, the kids are in bed, and we have the whole house to ourselves . . ."

Well, that's better.

"Now I'm going to tell you exactly what to do."

CHAPTER 32

A direct call

THREE WEEKS LATER, I have gone through my new lingerie wardrobe at least once. The kids in bed, we settle down in pajamas to a spaghetti dinner in our regular TV watching spots, me on the couch and Mark in the recliner. Yes, this is after some, well, effort. I pour him his favorite drink, rum and coke. He has the remote. Now is my best chance. Although Kevin said to not try it at home since Mark yelled the last time, I'm going to try and use some of the Dialog Wheel language and get to the bottom of Mark leaving Jonathan at the store once and for all.

I dig into the spaghetti. After a few bites, my hunger subsides and I put my bowl back in my lap, and begin.

"Soooo, I was puzzled by something . . . what do you think about all those times you lost track of Jonathan?"

Mark looks like he was slapped in the face. Hmm, maybe this wasn't the best plan.

Like knives thrown right back at me he says, "Um, **what exactly** are you talking about?"

Nice, it's like he conveniently forgot about the incidents. The last one was when? It has only been four months. I have to continue. So, I do, "I'm afraid of the possibility of Jonathan getting lost again when he's with you. Are you also?" I pick up my fork and take a thoughtful bite of my spaghetti. But what I get is . . . more knives.

"**Oh real nice,**" He stands up and so does his voice. "**This isn't about me. It's about the fact our son chooses not to listen to me. When are you just gonna let it go?**"

My stomach folds up. Maybe I should just be honest. "Well, I can't. I dunno. But what if you couldn't find him, then it would be your fault, right?"

"**What do you want me to do?**" He rumbles over me, like a volcano exploding. "**Drag him the next time? This is ridiculous, Heidi.**"

I can't speak. His face is red-mad. He rumbles over to the bathroom and I take my food and climb upstairs to the guest bedroom to watch some TV. To let him cool down.

What's going through my head during the rest of the hour while I unsuccessfully try to enjoy the TiVo'ed episode of *The Amazing Race*:

I can't let it go because *he* won't take any responsibility. How can *he* blame a three-year old? That doesn't logically make sense. He is an adult. And, even worse, a parent! We, he and I, have to take the *most* responsibility. To protect and serve our kids. If *he* can't admit his mistakes and apologize, instead of getting so goddam defensive about every single thing, how can he expect his kids to?

CHAPTER 33

A texted conversation

BEFORE GOING TO BED, and after three shows, I linger in the guest bedroom. Time to tell Mary what happened. I open up the slide keyboard on my phone.

Me: This just in from Lynn-land.

Mary: . . .

Me: Lynn has run away and is never coming back.

CHAPTER 34

Intimate Strangers
in the kitchen

TWO HOT, POOL-FILLED PLAYDATE SUMMER WEEKS go by in our new house. I go to bed early from the sun. We saw Kevin once; Mark didn't yell, and I didn't mutter sarcastic comments under my breath. Mark is not asking anymore about Lynn, and I'm not offering. Things seem peaceful, like the calm before a storm.

Until the Saturday before my birthday. I woke up craving my mom's family recipe of Swedish Meatballs. It has this sour cream gravy that I love. Yep, this recipe, for me, is very ambitious. It takes hours. And patience. That's why I need a weekend, I need Mark to cover the kids.

After a late breakfast of bacon, scrambled eggs, Entenmann's strawberry cream cheese coffee cake, and two potty breaks, I'm alone at the table with Mark. I hear the kids getting every toy down from the shelves in the toy room but that doesn't bother me. I have meaty goals to accomplish. Mark gets up from the table.

I clear the plates and say, "Hey, I was wondering if you could watch the kids this afternoon while I make my mom's Swedish meatballs?"

Mark's face twists shut and his lips purse. He points to his shirt. His words come out like little cigarette burns on my arm. My stomach already knows what the answer is.

"Why do you think I'm wearing my yard work shirt?" he begins, "For fun? I have to mow the lawn and edge and weed whack today. All of our neighbors mowed this week. The weekend is the only time I have to make our yard presentable because I have to go to work." He turns on his heel and leaves the room.

Why is everything so difficult with him?

"Yeah, okay, that's fine," I say, "No problem."

A familiar sinking feeling enters my heart. Why do I feel I always need an alternative-Daddy plan, because Daddy may not be available?

After a preliminary phone call to my mom, one more cup of coffee, and a run to the grocery store because I don't have beef bouillon cubes, I am ready to begin. I get Jonathan and Barbie set up with a new grocery-store present, a *Let's Go, Diego!* coloring book.

Two hours later, I have meticulously fried all but one side of one hundred meatballs in three pans without burning. BOOM, baby. The kids are now watching *Backyardigans*. I hear Mark coming downstairs after his shower. Finally, reinforcements.

He storms into the room, throwing his copy of *Intimate Strangers* on the floor. Fuck. I guess he's still angry about earlier. Puffed up like a peacock, he starts pecking at me.

"You know what your problem is? You keep looking for answers in damned books. You're not gonna solve any of our issues from a stupid book."

I see a flash of movement out of the corner of my eye. Before I can move, Jonathan is holding onto my leg, looking up. Barbie is close behind. Jonathan has the brow of an eighty-year-old. I kneel down and take both of their hands.

"Sweetheart, it's okay. Daddy and I are just sharing our feelings about a book from church." I reassure them. Jonathan looks at me, looks around my leg to Mark. I can feel Mark behind me, pacing like a caged tiger. I muster my mom-enthusiasm.

"Now, if you go back to your show in four seconds, you will get to watch another one after this," I say and hug them both.

They run back to their spot. I stand up and race-walk out of the kitchen, and hopefully out of earshot. Mark follows at my heels. I start talking in a fast whisper, hoping he matches my level.

"Do you remember that Kevin suggested *Intimate Strangers*? We both agreed that we would read it. I even took the crappy copy." I nod to my taped-up copy, sitting on the dining room table. Mark grows bigger, filling the room, pacing around the side of the table.

"Of course I remember. This book is bullshit."

Okay, this is my only chance to talk about the book. What did I learn that was so important? I speak with the lion ready to roar again in my face.

"First, I'm sorry you feel that way . . ."

Mark's eyes are black, dilated. He is ready to pounce on one wrong word. He's still listening, so there is hope.

"Second, I just feel like we don't have any emotional intimacy . . ."

Mark slices off my words like he's wielding a serrated knife, "**Just because you read it in some stupid fucking book, doesn't make it true.**"

I hold my hand up, "Yeah, I get that. But I *feel* like we are strangers. We don't share any actual feelings." Mark stops his pacing and puts his hands on his hips. Oh no.

"**Oh, real nice. I'd like you to prove that. Here's a real feeling, I feel like the book is bullshit.**"

He looks around wildly, like he's gonna find something and throw it at me. His eyes flash like obsidian reflecting a flame, his arm flies up, pointing at me.

"*YOU know what? YOU can talk about the book with Kevin. I'm done.*"

His voice over-inflates the room. I hear the door slam to the downstairs, to his video games. I look into the living room, both kids are standing up holding hands, wide-mouthed and staring at the basement door.

"It's okay. Daddy needs some Daddy time. And you two lucky little people, get another show!"

Looks like burnt meatballs for dinner.

CHAPTER 35
emotional intimacy

It's the years I haven't been able to cry in front of you.
It's the years I haven't been able to share my fears.
It's the years I haven't felt close enough
to look at you during sex.

It's the years that went by when you never
bothered to ask how I was.
It's the years that went by when you talked to me
with disrespect, impatience.
It's the years that went by when I was trying
to be your partner,
and, instead,
became your Mom.

CHAPTER 36

Thirty-four

FOUR DAYS LATER is my birthday. This year, my birthday greets me with heat. Which really isn't much of a surprise, since it's August in the Midwest.

I heave through my morning and get together a blow-up pool, slip and slide, water balloons, brownies, and homemade spaghetti sauce. This is more work than for my kids' birthdays. Maybe I should have invited my friends over to help me set up. That would have been a real birthday gift.

Instead, I shower a second time. Around lunch, Mary and a few preschool mom friends come. Soon our red and white checkered tablecloth is littered with half-finished dishes and Dollar Store 4th of July decorations.

After the kids go outside to play in the water, I refill the cups with Riesling. Thank God for fenced-in yards. I look around the table. All smiles. I knock my spoon against my plastic cup and stand up. I take a sip of my wine for courage.

"So, I'd like to make an announcement . . ." I start. My friends look up at me, puzzled. I continue, "I need to share something important, personal, with you all . . ." You could hear a pin drop. My heart beats in my throat.

"I'd like to let you know . . . Well, I have come to the conclusion that . . .

". . . I am a feminist."

Eruptions of laughter burst from the table; my brow furrows and my mouth hangs open in disbelief. Mary raises her glass.

"Well, of course you are!" she exclaims.

I look around the table.

"Heidi, you are one righteous bitch," another friend chimes in, "and now you know it, so you can own it! Look out, Mark!"

CHAPTER 37
Women of the Earth

How many goddam times
Do I have to hear
'Tired, exhausted, fine'
Come out of our mouths?
We cannot stand up for anything,
if we can't stand.

It is time,
my dears,
to burn his expectations.

What we are
is not a costume.
What we do
is not picked from a man-made menu.
How we love
is not the homemade in food.
And our worth
doesn't come from a jewelry box.

What we can achieve
is far greater than our imagination
if we give ourselves the goddamned permission
to find ourselves,
light our pyres,
sacrifice our own chauvinism.

Only then, we can
all rise from ashes
as Phoenix,
stronger,
ourselves,
together.

CHAPTER 38
The Shame Parfait

OVER THE NEXT couple of weeks, I go in for solo sessions with Kevin. Today is my third. Today, his office smells like fried chicken mingled with the sweet smell of prairie flowers, which are tall and blooming right outside his open window. The sun pelts against his wall of stained-glass windows, painting the room in patchwork color. I wonder if this is what being in a kaleidoscope feels like.

I love and dread coming. Kevin asks lots of different questions than in couple pastoral counseling. More direct questions. I never know how many times I'll have to excuse myself for the bathroom from nerves. But I feel so light, so free, after talking. Like I am stretching out my wings or something. So I keep coming.

"How are you today?" Kevin starts off the conversation. My heart leaps for joy. I can totally answer this one. I raise one hand up as if it's holding a platter.

"Well, on one hand, Jonathan is starting to learn his letters, and I'm teaching him how to tie his shoes." Then I raise my other hand platter-style, "And Barbie, she is trying to tie my shoes now that I'm teaching Jonathan. Which is hilarious, watching her drag my shoe around the house and roll it in between her hands like she's trying to spark a campfire."

I can see a tiny cloud of confusion descend from Kevin's brow.

"Heidi, that's great to hear. But what I meant to ask you is how are you feeling?"

Oh. I look down at my hands, never as long or slender as my Mom's. Hmmm. What. Am. I. Feeling? My fingernails always break right at the end of my fingertip. Never long enough to paint. Probably too many dishes. Shit, do I have enough clean plates for dinner?

Kevin breaks my worry-train with his comforting father voice.

"How about we pause and pray?" he asks.

"Dear God, thank you for this time for Heidi today. For her bravery to share what is on her mind and in her heart. May you guide her with your loving embrace. Amen."

For Heidi. I really like that.

"Amen. I'm sad." I say.

Kevin nods to me in understanding.

"Jonathan is gonna be going to kindergarten next year," I continue, "So, I locked myself in the bathroom yesterday so the kids couldn't see me . . . cry."

My heart fills up into my throat again, thinking of all that time away from my special little man. Some quiet moments pass. Kevin offers me Kleenex and I gladly receive it.

"Heidi, that's a good start."

"How is that good?" I challenge him. "Crying doesn't accomplish anything."

Kevin looks like he already has the answer this question. He looks up at the ceiling, then back down to me.

"You were made by a loving God. Your spirit. Everything. Even your emotions. He made you perfectly. And . . ." He takes a breath, continues, "So, you know we started talking about shame triggers?"

"How does that fit here?" Yep, I'm confused.

"When you were in the bathroom, did you, maybe, feel bad about crying? And that's why you hid from Jonathan and Barbara?"

Is he peering directly into my soul or something?

"Yes," I mutter.

His voice gets softer too, like he's soothing a scared horse.

"You feeling bad might mean that you feel ashamed of your sadness. When you get okay with feeling sad, then you can start to see other feelings you might have too. Feelings can be like a parfait."

But something inside of me automatically pushes back. Like he's getting too close to something. I need to stay open. To figure out what's going on. I don't want to cry in closed bathrooms forever. I want to be done with crying.

"But crying makes me feel so. Ummm. uncomfortable. Like I'm naked."

Kevin smiles his comforting smile, "Maybe vulnerable?"

I lean back and pause. Looking up at the stained-glass windows, I begin to piece my parfait together, trying to make the layers make sense.

"So, yeah, that's the word. *Vulnerable*. When I get really bristly when Mark starts accusing me of something, it's like I protect my vulnerable side from him. Like I put a top layer of defensive anger on my feelings-parfait." I pause. Yeah, that feels right.

I see the next layer unfold, "So what you're saying, is that when I feel bad, that's a shame layer. And when I'm sad about Jonathan, that's a sad layer. When I'm defensive, that's an angry layer. They're all feelings that I have to eat in my parfait or they get stuck in me. And when they can't come out, it's like I'm not feeling all the feelings God made me to feel?"

I look at Kevin. He's looking at me like I just gave the million-dollar answer.

"Wow, I could not have said that better myself. And, Heidi, please know you can't share your innermost feelings—your vulnerability—with everyone. It's not safe."

It's not safe echoes in my head and my whole body tingles. Holy shit, that means something.

"So Heidi, this week maybe you can try to do this," Kevin says. "when you feel bad, say to yourself 'It's okay to feel my feelings.' Then you can write them down in a safe place. Maybe next to your poems."

My stomach wrenches. My eyes widen and my shoulders rise.

"Aha! I felt it! I felt shame about you calling them poems. They're just my thoughts when I have a drink or two."

"Okay, that is real progress. Writing down your thoughts is a great way to start to understand your feelings-parfait. Because you are worth finding what makes you happy. What brings you joy." Kevin finishes, and smiles that big, beautiful, knowing smile of his.

Yeah, **I am** worth finding some joy.

CHAPTER 39

An abrupt ending

THE DAYS GO BY, and I feel stronger . . . more . . . alive-feeling, like something woke in me during my session with Kevin. Writing down the layers in my feelings parfait helps. Knowing my feelings, knowing when I'm ashamed, and feeling all that stuff, is some kind of big key.

I put the kids in their first morning preschool, three days a week. I cried to leave them. I wrote about me being sad and cried, then I felt better. Next, I noticed I was happy to drop the kids off at preschool. I wrote about that too. From writing, I was able to figure out that I felt happy to take me-time when the kids are at preschool. Normally I'd feel bad unless I was doing as many chores as possible. Now I feel good about taking a yoga class, writing, or going for coffee with a friend.

Today, after preschool, we all went over to Mary's house to hang out, and it was anything but happy.

So let me get you up to speed. Shortly after lunch, our kids had a rare disagreement over a toy. Things got bad enough that our 'mom-radars' were activated. After listening to her daughter's side of the story, Mary slammed her bedroom door right in my face! She didn't even ask me what I thought. I took my kids and left.

So now I'm home, sitting on my bed during the kids' naptime, crying. Thick, wailing-in-the-pillow cries. Kleenex surrounds me on my cream comforter like a graveyard of disfigured Smurf hats. The thing I really don't understand is that I've been crying for almost an hour now. I should be pissed at her, not sad. I don't understand. And, no, I don't feel like writing about it.

My phone rings. My heart sinks a little; it's not Mary, it's another friend. He's a bit older than me and pretty wise; he and I met several years ago through a young civic leader program, and we clicked right away. He is gentle and safe, kinda like the teddy bear I sleep with at night. It might be because he is the only dude I've ever met who openly shares his feelings and listens, instead of waiting his turn to man-splain. He and I don't hang out a lot because of our different schedules these days, but we call every so often to touch base. I get him up to speed. I hear him sigh.

"Heidi, you're sad because you like her."

Hello, Captain Obvious.

"Of course I do, she's my best friend!" I remind him, "She totally gets me."

Another sigh from the other end of the phone.

"No, Heidi, you really like her."

Again, I remind him, shaking my head, "Yes, I'm not going to pay twenty-five dollars for two Panera Salads for someone I don't like!"

There's a pause. Slowly, he continues, and presents each word like it's highlighted: "No, Heidi, you like her. Like you might be gay. Like you want to date her."

Oh, wow. I feel as though a line drive has knocked me upside the head from another country. My face flushes.

"Oh, uh, wow. Okaaaaay. I never thought about it that way," I stumble. For the first time in my life, I have no words. "Um, let's talk later, ok? I gotta go. And, uh, hey—thanks."

"Heidi?" His voice like a gentle bird alighted on my shoulder, "it's—you're—gonna be okay."

I hang up. I could go for that "everything's gonna be okay" blanket right about now.

I stand up from sitting on the bed. My head is quiet and numb, like I've just come out of a loud concert. I stare at the bed. The bed Mark and I have shared for a decade. The dark wood bed frame pushing me away, the cream comforter ready to muffle more tears, more years . . .

I think of my friend's words. Every piece of my skin feels cold, new, raw. Like I've just had my first shed after 34 years.

A stone appears in my stomach—that kind that settles in when you finally realize how long you've been walking in the wrong direction, and you can't make it back to camp by nightfall.

Oh fuck. I look down at my hands. That **could** explain my eternally-short fingernails.

CHAPTER 40
on hold

How long have I missed of me
and yearned for me?
About 34 years, give or take.
Resigned to grieving over
Hidden Heidi, for a while, at least, tho
I have a lot to do, time quickly filling
up my jar of sand with water, taking
the last of the volume.
I never thought I'd be so angry
and so sad
not at God,
or family,
or husband,
but myself.

CHAPTER 41

In the cramped office

I CANCEL MY NEXT TWO SESSIONS with Kevin, but I can't avoid him forever. Plus, he might know what to do. I can't believe this is happening to me. This whole notion of gayness is just ridiculous. But however much I write, I can't put this lesbian cat back in my bag. It keeps overfilling my feelings parfait. Back to Kevin I go.

I show up today in my hoodie, trying not to make eye contact. Next, I proceed to word-vomit the whole Mary story then ask Kevin what I should do. I fidget and teeter in my off-balance chair, like I'm a teen waiting for results from a pregnancy test that I already know the results of. He can make my constant self-berating go away. God, Heidi. How could you be so stupid? Now you have to suffer the consequences. Forever.

"Heidi, do you think that, maybe, you're bisexual?" These words come out of Kevin's mouth like a line drive from the Yukatan. I stop rocking my chair and almost fall off.

"Um, what does that even mean?" I am confused. Kevin continues, "Well, you've been married to Mark for over a decade. AND you seem to have strong feelings for your friend. You could like both men AND women."

"Oh God. Sorry. Really, is that a thing?" I have no idea.

"Yes. Bisexuals have their own letter in LGBTQ+" Kevin spells out those letters like he's in a spelling bee. Wow. I have no idea what the Q and + stand for. That's a question for another day. Back to my current situation.

"So, you don't think it's probably some normal thing that all women who have husbands *and* close woman friends go through?" I press him, hopeful. Kevin folds his hands in his lap and continues.

"How about you close your eyes and see if you can feel your answer."

I close my eyes and try to think about kissing the most attractive man. Harrison Ford? Legolas? Roy? My hands white-knuckle the chair arms, my forehead wrinkles, as if bracing for a wet-grandma kiss.

I picture kissing Mary. My body leans forward, relaxes, opens, flushes.

Goddammit, Heidi.

PART FOUR

THE POOL
OF TEARS

CHAPTER 42
Ping Pong

WEEKS GO BY and an urchin-like pokiness of shame fills my heart where apparently my budding crush for Mary was planted. I reach to pick up my phone to text her and check in, especially the day Jonathan learns to tie his shoes. But now, I hesitate.

Questions ping-pong in my head. Is she just a crush, or my best friend, or something more? Why would God do this to my closest relationship? Can she even continue to be my friend? In heterosexual land, you don't see married men hanging out alone with women who aren't their wives. Do the same rules apply in lesbian-land? When I see her next, can I be trusted to be alone with her—in pajamas, no less?

The kids have started asking to play with Mary's kids. I tell them that they are very busy and that we'll see them soon. I feel the same disappointment in their faces reflected in my poky heart.

I feel myself closing up, wilting, dying inside. Like if I don't reach out soon, my heart will permanently shrivel. I can't go back to that place.

So, I have made a decision. I am going to do what I'm really good at: I am going to layer up my feelings parfait and hide my awkward teenager-like feelings, because I need her friendship most of all.

CHAPTER 43

Time to fess up

ONE EVENING THE NEXT WEEK, I am back at Mary's house. Even though it's been a few quiet weeks, she opened her front door like no time had passed. God, I love that about Mary,

I grab a Stella from her fridge. She pours a glass of white wine, and we settle on her king-sized-bed-with-a-thousand-throw-pillows. I am showered and all made up, in a conservative pajama set. I keep telling myself that I'm gonna be okay. It's gonna be okay. She and I are gonna be okay.

She opens her laptop at the foot of the bed, in case there are any important Facebook updates. I sit quite a bit apart from her, just to be safe.

"So, there's something I need to talk to you about," I start. Mary stops mid-drink, reaches across the bed to put her hand on my thigh. Her eyes widen.

"Holy shit, Heidi, are you pregnant?"

"Hell No!" I laugh. "With Barbie finally free from her cloth training pants? No way am I going to sacrifice the decreased laundry load. *That* would be suicide."

I nod, Mary agrees. She leans back on her pillow and does an exaggerated wipe of her brow.

"Whew. So lady, what's up?"

Like ripping a band-aid right off, I straighten my back and look directly at her and say, "I am pretty sure I am gay." I close my eyes.

Please, please, please don't let her be mad. Please let it be okay. Please let her still be my friend. I hear Mary put down her wine. I open my eyes and see her arms go up like I made a goal.

"Hey! That's actually great! Your lack of satisfaction in the bedroom is finally solved!" Then her face darkens, she leans back over to me. "Oh no, what are you gonna do?"

"Well, I'm sure not gonna tell Mark. Do you think he could take Jonathan and Barbie away from me if he found out?" That is my biggest fear in the whole world.

"I dunno, maybe?"

I start to peel my beer label off. Well, good news is Mary is still my friend. Bad news is she doesn't have the answer.

"So," she interrupts my train of thought, "have you ever felt like dating a girl before? How do you know?"

Awkward. I take a big gulp of my beer. How to be honest here...

"Well, um, I was on the phone with another friend, and he said that he thinks that I'm probably gay. I've thought about it. And it pretty much makes sense—in theory."

I can tell the gears in Mary's head are turning.

"Heidi. This is unfortunate. However, theory isn't gonna cut it. I think we need to get you laid by a woman. To be sure."

She firmly nods her head like she's won the argument. I lean over. Is she gonna . . . Oh, no, she's looking for me to answer.

"I don't even know any gay women. And, to be honest, unless it involves Juliet, I don't even know what girl-on-girl action looks like."

Mary's face brightens. "I think it involves something like saran wrap."

We fall off her bed, laughing.

But despite the reconnection with my bestie, things grow quiet. Slow down. Like a cassette tape is caught in the deck . . .

CHAPTER 44

Nine months empty

Husband, ironing polo work shirts, swearing, cheering 'Da Bears.

Gramma, reorganizing linen drawers, *tsk tsk* under her breath.

Me-Wife, mixing chocolate chip cookies, red apple apron buttoned, tied.

Everything suburban,

expected, nuclear.

Except there is no love.

Except there is no me.

CHAPTER 45
Happy New Year

THE SUN WOKE ME UP today, a few days into the new year. Somehow, it found the sweet spot between the blinds and curtains and landed right on my eyes, like a middle-of-the-night toddler hand paddling me awake for a visit to the potty. I was really hoping for a sleep in. Oh well. I tend to avoid this dreaded day of the month; I mean, my monthly ~~swearing~~ sewing time.

I arranged for Mark to take the kids downstairs for an air-hockey tournament. It's win-win. Daddy gets X-Box time and the kids play air hockey instead of learning swear words from yours truly.

After breakfast I settle into the dining room. That overly perky winter sun is still streaming in. The warm-maple table that fits four of us and chairs with padded seats always makes me smile. Yeah, it's not fancy—more like a kitchen table—but the seats are comfy. We never really eat in here, so sewing is what I do at the table other than clean my china.

The bonus is that the dining room seems to be the warmest place in the house in winter, and it has a recessed ceiling that gives off different geometric shadows depending on the time of day. My daughter loves watching the shadows, and the beige plush carpeting makes it library-quiet . . . I sometimes feel like this house was made for me to get too comfortable in so I forget. Everything.

No time to shadow-watch today. I fold away our white damask tablecloth and lug my sewing machine suitcase and sewing basket onto the table. I take a deep breath, roll back my shoulders a couple times, and crack my neck side-to-side. I got this.

Today's challenge is cuffs around Jonathan's grey and maroon fleece pants.

Five minutes in, it begins. I get my first giant knot that causes me to respool bobbin thread. Dammit. Dammit. Why did I have to use the cheap thread? My stomach tightens. My shoulders creep closer to my ears.

Eight minutes in, I press down on the pedal and my sewing foot refuses to move. There's just this buzzing noise, like when people get buzzed into a building. I only changed cuffs. What's the big deal? Why is there a different issue *every-fucking-time* I use this thing? If there's a Hell for me, it will include sewing machines.

That's it. I'm done. I stand up. Yeah, I fucking give up! I quit!

I can't even sew a circle around a stupid loop of fabric. I am like the pant leg that won't be tamed by any sewing machine. I'm too long and am going to drag around behind my son and get all torn and dirty, and then I'll trip him all the time.

I slump to the floor behind the table and start to cry. Okay Heidi, you know what to do. Better in than out. All I can think is if I divorce Mark, I will ruin my kids' lives.

NO booms into my head like Kevin's shouting at me.

Startled, I wipe my eyes and look around the room. I listen to the house. Only the muffled noise of the video game and air hockey table meets me. I stare into the adjoining toy room. My mind continues to punch at me.

I have failed my kids. Failed. Failed. Failed. My hands go to my face, and I cry. After a while, I get quiet. I sit back against the dining room wall and close my eyes.

In my mind, I see Mark, holding up a sign: Fear, Anger, Offense, and Shame. I look down at what my arms are holding. My sign says Fear, Anger, Defense, and Shame.

We are mirrors of each other, oil and water laying in a glass that will never dissolve.

We have both failed the kids.

gagged

I stand fully before you
arm extended, flexed
finger pointing
YOUR fault
How could you?
Time to put you in the ring
with the wild animals
as that is what you are.
But feeding you,
quietly, gagged by my own hands,
nourishing your tone, values, authority,
laying next to you,
night after night,
I look in the mirror:
Wild animal I have become.

CHAPTER 47

3:32 AM

SEVERAL QUIET WEEKS LATER...

NOT SAFE not safe not safe   not safe   not safe

Booms at me like a bad-80s-movie echo. I shoot up in bed, my heart like I've been running too fast. All I can see are the street-light-illuminated white walls and the red numbers 3:32 on our clock. I shove Mark's shoulder.

"Hey, Mark. Did you hear that?" I whisper.

Mark groans. I persist.

"Did you just hear that?" I whisper and shake his shoulder. Mark rolls over on his back, leans his head up.

"No."

Weird.

"Okay, sorry for waking you. Just a bad dream, I guess." Though I'm sitting up in bed, when I close my eyes I feel like I'm falling. I stare at the clock to steady myself and my racing heart.

I Am Not Safe.

I'm not emotionally safe. My kids are not physically safe. Mark is not changing; he's like a loose cannon. I'm waiting around here, hoping that he will change. Someone is going to end up lost, or hurt, if I don't do something.

My body tingles at this. The same tingle I had in Kevin's office when he said not everyone is safe to be vulnerable with. I feel safe enough to close my eyes. I feel the large, looming monster stepping out of the shadows into the light. She is a large mama bear, complete with do-rag and apron, there to protect me from falling over the edge. From a fall so steep I could not, would not, survive. That's what she was trying to do. Trying to let me know I'm not safe, trying to protect me. She comes over and envelops me with her soft, comforting warmth. Then evaporates, like ash, leaving her do-rag in my hands. I open my eyes. I am the mama bear now.

My vision and heart slowly steady, like waves lapping after a storm. I exhale a breath I feel I've been holding for years, and go downstairs to get a glass of warm milk.

I come up with a three-step plan, and I memorize it.

I imagine there is a wall between Mark and I in bed, so I move as far away from him as possible before trying to fall asleep. Like a mama bear mummy.

CHAPTER 48
STEP 1:
Be My Guest

ABOUT AN HOUR LATER, I sneak out of bed and greet Jonathan on his. God, I am so grateful he can now wait until the clock hits six-something before waking me up. It's been almost five years of sunrise wake-up calls.

He and I go down to the kitchen and, with the help of a foot stool, he helps me make coffee and oatmeal for breakfast. Man, he's getting so tall.

About an hour later Mark comes downstairs, dressed for work. After a brief waltz-hug, he purses his lips. Oh no, what now?

"Have you seen my travel mug?" Which in Mark-language means "what did you do with my mug?" But this tired lady is not in the mood.

"Sorry, no. Maybe it's at work?"

"I am sure I gave it to you yesterday after work," he presses.

I turn to offer him my mug as a peace offering, and wince. One hand holding the counter, the other gripping my lower back. Mark's expression changes to surprise.

"Are you okay?"

"No. I'm fine. It's just that my back has been hurting me in the mornings," I lie. "I think I'm gonna relocate to the guest room futon to see if it's our mattress." Mark's face softens as he gathers up his coffee in my mug.

"Okay, call me at work if you need me to pick you up some meds or anything."

I think Step One went pretty well.

CHAPTER 49

STEP 2:
Early Learning

A COUPLE WEEKS INTO my guest room futon experiment, I talk with Mark about the second and third steps of my plan: daycare for kids and a job for me. I know he's always been nervous about being the sole breadwinner, so he is all in for steps two and three.

Oh yes, my back is better. No, Mark hasn't asked about me coming back to the bedroom.

A week later, the kids and I walk into a wandering mid-century-modern-mansion-now-a-daycare. Each wide room is flanked by a wall of windows on one side and endless shelves of colorful toy bins on the other. It smells like playdoh and kids. Much better than that last place that smelled like diapers, dirty ones.

The mulched backyard has a giant wooden pirate ship treehouse and lots of other nooks and crannies to explore. Both Jonathan and Barbie release their death grips on my hands and run to explore the outside. Well, that's a good sign.

Then a battle begins. A battle I've carefully avoided for almost five years. A battle, I know, will keep me quiet and at home, because there's shame layered all over it.

Imagine me with a miniature llama on each of my shoulders. The first is a miniature beige llama, is wearing a 1950s housewife apron, perfectly coiffed hair, and red fingernails. She carries with her a dust mop, a well-behaved child on one hip, and to-do lists. We shall call her *Traditional Heidi*. Traditional Heidi words layer on like thick frosting, with resentment and sarcasm. She likes waggling her finger at people and muttering things under her breath.

On my other shoulder is a miniature rainbow colored llama, with long dreads and a flowy Holly Hobby patchwork skirt. She is *Feminist Heidi*. She comes complete with a bow and arrow, a couple of pom-poms, and a journal. She speaks freely and positively of body, mind, and spirit. She is herself unto no one. She gets enough sleep, and she is unafraid to speak her truth.

I'm in the middle. My inner battle begins.

"Well, if I was a little kid, this place would be a wonderland!" Feminist Heidi starts.

Traditional Heidi rolls her eyes and shakes her head.

"Heidi never went to daycare. Her mom stayed home the whole time, which meant lots of homemade chocolate chip cookies and homework help." Feminist Heidi is unfazed.

"Heidi can still do cookies and homework. And Jonathan and Barbie will make so many new friends here," Feminist Heidi says without fear. This only aggravates Traditional Heidi; she stamps her front hoof in disapproval.

"But the kids will be so tired from being away from home all day. All because Heidi doesn't care about them as much as her *plans*."

Feminist Heidi nods her head in agreement and continues, cool as glass, "Yes, the kids are going to be tired.

138

But Heidi will love them and find her own way. Would you rather have the kids unsafe with Mark all the time?"

Traditional Heidi pauses while writing down items on her to-do list, barely lifts her head, and mutters a reply.

"They would be safe if Heidi just tried to Mother Hen again." Each word from Traditional Heidi is baited for guilt. Feminist Heidi is undeterred.

"Heidi can't sacrifice her whole life to their safety. Especially when she's not safe, either. Kevin said that Heidi needs to put on her air mask in the airplane *before* theirs. Which means a j-o-b," Feminist Heidi responds.

Traditional Heidi pauses for a minute, purses her lips, and goes in for the kill, like a beater pummeling my heart.

"Heidi will never be like her mom."

Traditional Heidi's words take my breath away. I stand, frozen, looking at the daycare playground.

Feminist Heidi does a magnificent full-body shake, a deep down-dog stretch, sits down, and scribbles some things in her journal. Then she begins.

"Yes, you are right. Heidi cannot be her mom. She is a different mom. And that doesn't make her a bad mom. Or a selfish mom. How about this idea; if things get bad, she will get a nanny instead of the daycare. Deal?"

"Deal," brays Traditional Heidi, and writes it down on her to-do list.

I sniff back tears. Jonathan and Barbie are running around the giant pirate ship treehouse, laughing.

I turn to the daycare director.

"They get time to nap every afternoon, right?" The director nods affirmative.

"Great, we're in."

CHAPTER 50

evergreen

STARING AT THAT PIRATE SHIP TREEHOUSE got me curious. I've been spending a lot of time in my guest bedroom after the kids are asleep. Sometimes I write, sometimes I sleep for twelve hours. Sometimes I look out my single, tiny window at the other rooftops and trees in my view until it's dark.

But today is different. This week, my windows are the dining room windows. My parents are visiting, and I have given them the guest bedroom. I am sleeping in the dining room. It's actually quite cuddly, if you want to know.

This weekend morning I pretended I was asleep until they all left. Mark up and out early, golfing with buddies. My parents planned a day of park visits, hot dogs, and ice cream with Jonathan and Barbie. Which is great, because Jonathan won't be so nervous about me leaving his sight with the grandparent-minute-men around.

After the door slams, I slowly un-cocoon from my sleeping bag, stretch up, and feel the sun rays from the windows filter through my fingertips. Ahhh warmness. A few minutes later I pull the blinds open, and sit wrapped in my robe embracing a steaming cup of coffee.

Today is glorious. It's the first warm day of early Spring. One of those days when you can go for a discovery walk and see the crocuses and daffodils peeking out from the ground. The kids LOVE touching the new buds and plants. Their eyes widen; their chubby hands are so gentle with the new life.

Today is wide open. But is it? My brain keeps reminding me of that pirate ship treehouse, and other questions keep knocking around in my head like bouncy balls. Do I *have to do* the same thing every day? And Keith's question: What brings me joy?

I throw on a pair of old jeans, lace up my tennis shoes, and grab the car keys.

Fifteen minutes later I pull up to a bustling local park, one I am sure they did not go to. The playground is mobbed; I park on the other side and get out. There's about a half mile of paved walking path around the park, but I'm not here to walk today. My eyes scan the landscape, looking for the perfect one.

Tree, I mean.

I spy a robust evergreen. I duck under the lowest boughs to get closer and am immediately met by a glorious smell that brings me back to childhood trips to my cousins' house in the Rocky Mountains. I close my eyes and feel the scent diffuse and relax my entire body. Delicious.

It's probably a young evergreen tree; about two of me would be able to encircle the trunk. It has long needles and branches. I stand at the base and look up; sunlight pierces in spots through the neural-network of branches to highlight the dusty brown bark.

Okay Heidi. Are you ready? I do little jumps up and down, roll my shoulders, and crack my neck side to side, like I'm getting ready for a boxing match.

I spy a branch that is just lower than shoulder height. Let's do this. My hands encircle the branch like a sloth and I jump off the ground. I heave my chest up, my left leg gets over . . . and around the branch. I cling like a scared cat on the top side of the branch. Wow, I did it. I thought I'd have at least a couple faceplants. I pull up to a seated position. Time to get to work.

I look up and survey the network of branches. I find a branch that's within reach. I pull myself up. And again. And then again. I feel calm, resolved, strong.

A couple of carefully planned minutes later, and before the branches get dangerously thin, I sit. I think this will do. I wish Jonathan and Barbie could see me now! Oh wait, maybe not; it would give them ideas. Maybe I'll tell the kids when they're older, like forty.

I look at my hands which are sticky and scratched from my climb. I wipe them on my wrecked jeans. I notice a spot of sunlight has settled on my chest. I close my eyes and breath in. I feel the sun warm my heart. Wow.

Then my gaze draws outward.

HOLY SHIT. I am almost fifteen feet off the ground. I didn't realize how far up I went. But then, I am still calm. None of my I'm-afraid-of-heights triggers are going off. WTF?

What am I feeling? I feel safe. I feel joy. I feel brave. I could live up here.

I look out through the branches and see the busy walking path. I watch as walker after runner after stroller come and go, always on the paved, circular sidewalk. Not one person venturing off. They even seem happy about it! It's easier walking on the concrete, after all. But you know what? The sidewalk is only about two percent of the park. They don't even know they are missing ninety-eight percent of the park by following someone else's path.

Time for this bitch to go off-road and find the other ninety-eight percent of her life. I laugh out loud.

CHAPTER 51
mother

Here I am.
I didn't think I could do it,
but I tried anyway,
and I did.
Three-times-Me height off the ground,
palms sticky from sap, and
feet dangling in free air.
Held.

Protected by Her,
Surrounded by Her
steadfast smell and
magnificent petticoat of
Evergreen as she
shelters me,
if just for a moment, from the
radically changing weather in my life.

From my cradle, I
watch Not One deviate
from the paved park path. I
laugh, my path is never again
paved, now requires some
climbing shoes,
a lot of bandages.

My growing compass of light
within points me higher still,
to a, my, new, beautiful
Mother.

CHAPTER 52
STEP 3:
Welcome to The Club

THE SUMMER is only half over, but it's over for me. This morning I dropped the kids off at their new daycare, cried in my car, reapplied makeup, and went to my first day of work. I saw no sun or summer fun as I have been inside all day. How do people do this every day? My only solace is that I can mark step three off of my to-do list.

It is the end of the day. I sit with air-conditioning cold hands in front of an abnormally large desk in front of an abnormally large bookcase in a small office. Shelves are lined with pictures of locally famous people, like the mayor. The Country Club Manager's office. My Spanx and throbbing feet in my tall heels are a welcome distraction from the overbearing office. My manager looks up from his papers and folds his hands on his desk.

"So, Heidi, how was your first day?"

Normally I would share every single thing, but this is my manager. I'm here for positivity and brevity.

"I am so honored to be here," I respond. "To help serve the members. And everyone here is so nice!"

My manager sits back in his chair and rubs his hand on his chin. He is a middle-aged, middle-height, middle-hairline man whose reputation precedes him: recently divorced, married to his job, working the board of directors like he's up for election, volatile. If I worked all the time, I'd be pretty spicy too.

I hold my breath, hoping for no more questions like the interview: do I have a husband, what does he do, and why do I want a job if I like being a homemaker? His eyes feel like Superman's, they can see through anything. One of his hands hovers up over his mouth.

"Great, well, I look forward to working with you. Welcome to the Club," he says from behind his hand. I am unnerved about him covering his mouth when he speaks. Why does he do that? What is HE hiding?

We stand up and shake hands and then I leave. I hop in Miss Daisy, light as a feather. This job is mine, for better or worse. Time for a drink with Mary.

pixie cut

Why do we wear these blinds
pulled distractingly-long
curled, tressed?

The light within us,
so deeply, properly,
curtained by our
Pantene-luscious locks.
You do love them, don't you?

Are you afraid to see us,
unshaded from within?
The blinding brilliance of our spirit,
our muchness, strong as yours.
Your objectifying,
generations entrenched,
holding them long, I get it.

Well, they are gone.
No more hands
on my blinds.

Pixie opens
Eyes bright as the sun.

CHAPTER 54

Thirty-five

A COUPLE WEEKS after starting my job is my birthday. I find myself in a modern wine bar, after dark. The heat of August follows me in, but the air-conditioning envelopes my body like a walk-in beer cooler. Delicious.

Long 1960s-style white leather bench seats on one side are contrasted against a charcoal wall, breaking high against a repainted tin roof ceiling. There are heavy lacquered tables, and an up-lighted bar casts a blue glow like Austin Powers' bedroom.

Mary, a few Mothers and More moms, and a couple of church friends surround me. A beautiful motley crew of middle-aged Midwest mommas. Strappy tops and makeup, no tracksuits or mom-ponytails in sight. We look so different, maybe more ourselves? Maybe more awake? Maybe that's the makeup.

Nestled in the middle of a white bench seat with two Rieslings coursing through my veins, I look around. I am holding one friend's hand, and another has her arm around my shoulders.

"So, my big boy Isaac totally didn't suck when tried to breastfeed him! I mean, he could barely find my nip. Hell-o, it's right there!" One friend says, pointing to her chest, and the entire table bursts out laughing. She continues, "Aren't babies born with a radar for food? You see all those baby calves, gettin' right down to business."

More laughing.

I have never felt this way. This . . . connected. I have friends. I am not alone. It's not just me anymore, struggling through mommyhood, shouting into an empty universe, feeling *just fine*. I gratefully look at Mary. I could not have opened up to these other mommas without her support.

I hold up my wine glass and stand. Someone clinks theirs.

"Thank you all, beautiful friends, for coming tonight. I love all of you. And I'm sorry I haven't seen you as much as usual, being a working woman now. You all coming is the best gift I could receive. You are my family. So, in true Heidi fashion, I wrote you a poem . . ."

CHAPTER 55

a mes amies

A birthday toast
to those I love.
Thanks to you
who joined me on my walk.
You have
Shown me trust is possible,
even when I don't trust myself,
Let me nurture you from my kitchen,
even while the food wasn't good,
Shared your fragility
so I can share mine,
Shown me how to live presently,
while the future seems steep,
Guided me to deeper waters
with patience of a saint.
But, mostly,
thank you for the smile in my heart,
whenever I gaze upon yours.
Salut, mes amies.

CHAPTER 56

In the Drawer

I'VE BEEN AT MY JOB A MONTH. I can honestly say I like working at the Country Club. I am the new Membership and Marketing Manager, also known as the public face of the Country Club. Which seems a bit odd they would pick someone who's never been a member to help bring in new members? But welcoming people and making them feel comfortable is one of my two superpowers. My other superpower is writing thank you notes. So, between a mutual friend's recommendation and my superpowers, I got the job.

My workplace—the Club—is so fancy. It reminds me of a green and gold carpeted conference center. Right when you walk in, you encounter a this-is-supposed-to-be-a-living-room-with-a-fire-that's-never-lit, ringed by stiff, uninviting furniture, breakout rooms, and a lovely Beaut-and-the-Beast-worthy ballroom. There is so much crown molding I'm pretty sure they dismantled the Queen Mary to make it. The only downside of the fanciness is I have to dress up. Every day. No track suits allowed.

The office has a totally different atmosphere, though. There are seven people who work within 15 feet of each other. Clearly some lack of foresight. but I like chatting, so

I'm good. However, I have heard my boss yells at serving staff. So, there's that.

To top it all off, there's one other thing that's different from my previous gigs.

It's called a *Worry Drawer*. When I get to work, I put my angry-at-Mark, I'm-confused-about-my-lesbianness, sad-about-leaving-kids-at-daycare parts in my worry drawer. Woke up crying? Tears pour in. Worrying about money? There's a file for that. My dad often said when I was young: "Shields up, Heidi. Time to go to work."

Kevin would probably say it's unhealthy, hiding my feelings in a drawer. This is what I have to do right now. AND . . .

I have a *Breathing Drawer* to combat the effects of the Worry Drawer. It contains band-aids for high-heel blisters, chocolate, graham crackers, notes from Mary, family, and friends so I remember I am loved; and some weird gingerbread tea that I don't like, but that someone gave to me for Christmas, and I don't want to waste it.

I feel my Worry and Breathing Drawers will balance each other, eventually.

CHAPTER 57
cables

A blessed life, intertwined
between us three.
Love, patience, laughter:
Mommy and her two baby bears.
Braided stronger than steel cables.
Welded together by Him/Her, Love.
The distance,
through demand of
Occupation and
through dream of
no longer wanting to be
nowhere in her own life,
cables-strained, tear-stained
tensile-tested.
night
after
day
after
night
wondering what all the stress is worth.
Further from my lights, myself,
than I ever was.

CHAPTER 58

It's not you, it's me.

THAT SUNDAY EVENING, after getting the kids down, I retire to my guest room. I sit on the edge of my futon, staring at these lines on the back of my Church bulletin written by a Jewish prisoner in a Nazi concentration camp.

> "I believe in the sun
> even when it is not shining
> And I believe in love,
> even when there's no one there.
> And I believe in God,
> even when God is silent."

I look up, out of my window. A small window with tiny blinds rolled up, looking west to the end of a day of summer thunderstorms. Why did I pick a house with such tiny windows?

I stare at the fading light.

The Jews' pain was a tsunami to my teaspoon. They were in a death camp. They knew it was only a matter of time. That their light was fading. And they chose hope.

Hope can be my choice. All I need to do is believe; and then I will make things happen. I've already done the first three steps . . . maybe some hope will get me to the next one.

CHAPTER 59
Meanwhile

A T WORK THE NEXT WEEK, my eyes float across the office to a narrow, encumbering, converted filing room. In front of a counter lay several five-inch binders and two laptops; and sometimes, two more coworkers, the event planners.

Okay, Heidi. Today's the day.

It's been six weeks since I started. The kids are loving their daycare, and I've already got two new friends in the office. But this Stacey person—one of the planners—I haven't talked with her at all, which isn't too weird because someone told me she broke her ass setting up an event right when I started. Now it makes sense why she carries around a toilet-seat-shaped pillow.

She's like a little butterfly, stopping here and there, flower to flower, coordinating events, with her shoulder-length strawberry blonde hair and a colorful scarf tailing behind her. She seems the most efficient event director on the planet.

But I think she's also very shy, which makes me very curious. Introverts always make me curious, with their unknown depths. I get up, smooth my soft brown shift, check the buckles on my heels, and begin my ten-foot walk.

Then, the lanky could-be-my-son Assistant Club Manager strides into the office, straight into Stacey's, blocking my route.

Oh well. I quickly pivot to the copy machine and pretend to look through the printed stack.

I peek to see him leaning over, talking quietly. Her usual unreadable face bursts into laughter and light. She's gotta be at least a decade younger than me.

And she flutters away to coordinate another event.

CHAPTER 60
Capsize

A FEW DAYS LATER I walk in barefoot, heels in sweaty hands from a three-story climb, through a different therapist's waiting room to her office.

Yeah, I decided to get a real, licensed, knows-what-it's-like-to-be-gay therapist. I might as well have someone who can understand at least half of the stuff making me a headcase, because I'm not addressing the lesbian-elephant in the room.

This is my third visit. I think I'll be able to share today. A mismatched-Goodwill-furniture-kinda-comfy-room, unpretentious and calming. I sit down and put my shoes in my purse. She gives me an 'it's okay, I understand your foot pain' nod, and my eyes are drawn up, again.

There's this framed drawing I keep staring at in her office. It is showing up in my dreams now; I can't shake it. It's a drawing of a person wrapped like a mummy with their hands covering their face. I feel like that person every day. I can't resist, I need to know. I point to the drawing.

"So, what is that mummy drawing all about?" I ask.

My therapist's soft, well-lined face softens as she says, "Shame."

My whole body recognizes that word. Tears start forming in the corners of my eyes. That's the layer in my feeling parfait that I am avoiding and don't want to eat.

"I feel so much shame about not knowing that I am gay."

I look down at the industrial carpet. As I exhale, my heart grows heavy. I don't feel like I deserve to inhale. Tears pour out as from a broken dam, and my inhale catches. I cover my forehead. I grab a bunch of Kleenex with shaking hands. I cry and choke up and cry.

I cannot tell how much time passes. Time drags on my heart and limbs like I have been thrown into a lake, and I have sunk to the lifeless bottom and am ready to gather algae.

I sniff up the last of my tears and wipe the raccoony-mascara mess that I am sure is my eyes. My therapist begins with the gentleness of someone opening my curtains to wake me on a soft morning.

"Heidi, how do you feel now? Do you feel like sharing?"

My answer comes quickly, "Well, I guess I'm proud of myself for crying in front of you. But I also feel ashamed about wanting to get divorced. And for being a different person than I thought I was. I feel like, between both of these things, I'm going to ruin the lives I love the most instead of save them."

I sink back to the lifeless bottom of the lake, and the tears recommence.

CHAPTER 61
2:17am

2:17AM THAT NIGHT, I stare at my bedroom ceiling, unable to sleep. I pull Mr. Bear closer into the crook of my arm. Yes, I've adopted a teddy bear to sleep with since the master bedroom move-out. Scruffy light brown Illini Bear has been a God-send.

But even he can't help me now.

God, **HOW COULD YOU DO THIS TO ME?** Why would you make me gay and a mom? Being a mom is, like, the only thing I'm mildly good at. I feel Mark could take the kids away from me if he found out I'm gay. If Jonathan and Barbie are not in my life...

CHAPTER 62
No Green Eggs

I cannot be
gay, as I am.
I cannot be me,
Sam I am.

Not in this house.
Not with this spouse.
Not at my job.
Thrown out in the turn of a knob.
At Junior League?
That already gives me PTSD.

And my kids. Oh my kids!
Well, what would they think?
Future confusion and doubt
only make my heart sink.

I cannot be
gay, as I am.
Maybe I cannot be,
Sam I am.

CHAPTER 63
leadening

I WAKE UP EACH DAY for the next ten days, body a sandbag on my futon bed. I don't want to.

CHAPTER 64

Lost

I never gave my heart to him,
because it never was my heart.
And when it was his love that came,
I could never feel it,
because it never was my heart.

I thought I gave my soul to them
but I never knew my soul.
And when it was myself who came,
I could never see her,
because a stranger was my soul.

PART FIVE

WONDERLAND

CHAPTER 65

quitter

ON THE ELEVENTH MORNING, I wake up with a different feeling. I lay still, keeping my eyes closed. A vivid scene, like a Polaroid picture, presents itself front-and-center in my mind. It's from a dream, I know it. A scene from two decades earlier. I'm 12 years old.

I'm on one side of our kitchen pass-through window, and my dad is on the other. My dad: my tutor, soccer coach, our all-around fix it guy, the main driver on vacation. He's not as German-American as my mom, but what I do, I do so he can be proud: Straight A's. Clubs. Saving babysitting money for college. I'm the only daughter. His sweetheart.

I'm dressed in sweats, hair ponytailed in a royal blue and white trucker baseball hat. My dusty softball glove thrown on the counter.

My dad talks as if writing in permanent ink, "This is it. This is the only time you get."

My pre-teen whine runs over any chance of a logical-sounding answer, "But the girls are mean. Every practice is the worst. And, when Becca's mom comes to practice and yells, the coach just lets her pitch. She isn't even good."

My dad continues with his permanent-ink declaration, "Okay. But this is the only time you get to quit." Something clicks inside of me. Yes.

Yes, this is worth that one chance.

"Dad, you got yourself a deal. No more quitting." We shake hands through the window.

I am not a quitter.

CHAPTER 66

The rundown

A T THE END OF WORK that day, I look out my office window at the Country Club. Stacey is **finally** leaving work before me. I grab my bowling-bag-of-a-purse and semi-run down the circle drive, almost breaking my ankle in my leopard-print high heels. Is a new friend worth an ankle? Maybe.

I get within earshot of Stacey and place my hands on my hips to recuperate.

"*Hey, Stacey*! Just wanted to introduce myself. I'm Heidi." My Spanx remind me that heavy breathing is a no-no.

She answers, her voice as calm as Walden's Pond, But she's looking at my hands like she expects something to be in them. "Yeah, I know. Nice to meet you. Did I forget something at the office?"

Oh, yeah, she probably thinks I'm crazy or something. Running after her.

"Um . . . no. I just like to get home quickly." Her face relaxes, and she turns to walk to her car.

"Okay, well, have a good night," she says. Oh no, not again. I start talking to her back.

"Hey, um, I just wanted to ask you if you'd maybe like to catch lunch sometime?"

CHAPTER 67

The Bread Co

EARLY THE NEXT WEEK, mismatched tables, a four-sided fireplace, and the smell of freshly-baked bread meet us as we enter a local sandwich shop. It has this laid-back-granola-college-kid vibe. And Swiss bread. Every time I come here I wonder how they bake the cheese into it.

We order, then settle into the only tiny table left, with off-balance iron chairs that feel like discards from someone's patio.

Stacey is wearing tan slacks, a pressed white no-frills short-sleeve blouse, and a spring green scarf, which brings out the warmth in her strawberry blonde hair. I wonder if she's part Irish or something? Her freckled face is quiet. Man, she has a poker face for life.

But I'm so excited. New people to me are like presents. It sounds cheesy, but every person I meet is a gift to me. Especially after not having many people in my life for a long time.

"So, thanks for coming! This will be nice," I bubble over with excitement.

Stacey continues her poker face, taking a sip of water.

"Yep, no problem."

"How's work going today?" I ask.

Stacey's voice becomes more like flat soda, "It's work. Like a job."

"So, this isn't, like, your life's calling?" I say, with a wink.

As if handing me roadkill with ten-foot tongs, she replies, "Definitely not."

So, she's doesn't like event planning, hmmm . . . Stacey pauses and gives me an answer that sounds like a broken record.

"I dunno what I'm supposed to do with my life." Her eyebrows raise, "What about you?"

"Well, first thanks for asking. And I have no idea, either. I am just at the Club because . . . well, things aren't great at home. I mean, with my husband. I mean, he's a great provider. But in the *Dad* and *feelings* and *communications* categories, he has room for improvement, which he doesn't want to explore. Anyway, this job is great because all the Club Members are super nice, and it seems they actually need this kind of social network. You know?"

"I guess so. I never thought about the Club that way," Stacey replies.

"So, how long have you been at the Club?"

"I started as waitstaff and have worked my way up. So about two years," she says. I start to feel it's going to be impossible to get Stacey into something other than a one-liner for an answer. She is one tough cookie. Or I need to change topics.

"So, what did you do before?"

"I was in the Air Force. And I've lived in a few cities around the country doing jobs to make enough money until I move again. And to travel."

That word *travel* lights up her face. Aha. That's what she really likes.

We are interrupted by the arrival of our sandwiches and chips. I look down at a beautiful plate. I am overjoyed.

"This sandwich looks great!" I point to her plate, "Thanks for the suggestion! That's great that you have seen so many cities. Mark and I don't travel unless we are visiting family. And we lived in Austin, Texas for three years before we moved back closer to family so we could have kids. I really miss the breakfast burritos and brisket. That's so great that the Club has opportunity for advancement. I've always worked at small places where I am the one person in my department. Like the black fundraising sheep who has nowhere else to go. And the board never listens to that person, anyway. I always seem to end up in places like these with the exact same salary. And difficult bosses. Holy Cow!"

I pause and gape at Stacey. She's already finished half of her sandwich and there is nary a crumb on her plate, or her face. She looks up.

"I haven't taken a bite and you already finished half of your lunch!" I exclaim.

Fast eating would solve the mystery of why I've never seen her in the lunchroom at work. My stomach reminds me I need to eat, too. I take a deep bite. Oh yeah, this is the sandwich I've been looking for. Oh shit. Hot raspberry juices start dripping down my chin onto my lap. I only have two tiny paper napkins. I don't even think Stacey has a blemish on her one. I tilt my chair back to reach the napkin dispenser and take out a good two-inch chunk, and start to wipe. After a minute, I feel confident enough to continue, and Stacey reminds me I still have jelly streaked on the side of my cheek. I laugh.

"Thanks. Your tidiness is so impressive. I bet you do really well at lunch interviews. Sometimes I end up with barbeque sauce on my inner thigh—an unfortunate area—or butter across my chest. My family made fun of me growing up. Maybe I just need to wear a lobster bib all the time. I'm sure the Club would love their Membership and Marketing Director suiting up in plastic."

Stacey and I both smile. What is that word when you don't feel bad about learning how to do things? Oh yeah, Kevin told me it was humility. I have humility about my eating challenges.

I get a quarter of the way through my sandwich, eat the chips, decorative lettuce, and call it quits. I will finish it at home, before I change to come back to work.

CHAPTER 68

Prayer of Illumination, Islamic

O God, give me a light in my heart,
And light in my tomb,
And light in my hearing and light in my sight
And light in my feeling and light in all my body,
And light before me and light behind me,
And light on my right hand and light on my left hand,
And light above me and light beneath me.
O Lord, increase light within me, and give me light,
and illuminate me.
I sleep with this prayer from last week's Church
service bulletin, under my pillow.

Seven Saints

IT'S ONLY BEEN a week or so since our lunch, and Stacey and I have been texting. A LOT. Even more than I chat with Mary. I knew Stacey would be an interesting person, once I got inside her introverted-walls, that is. But, a worry is growing.

I haven't told her that I'm gay. And, if she's going to be my friend, she has to know. I'm gonna do it in person. It's the best way.

After getting the kids down one night, I get ready and drive downtown to our Irish pub. I walk inside and am immediately attacked by mirrors. Why beer companies make their signs out of mirrors, I will never understand. I see Stacey, who already has a drink; she gives me the nod to get my own.

Time to get this over with. I pay for a Rogue Dead Guy ale and slide opposite her in a large corner booth. She has a rust color leather coat, matching her freckles, and an understated pink floral camp shirt underneath, highlighting her cheeks. Her spring blue eyes sparkle. Like when she laughs.

Best do it now, so I don't get too deep in friends-ville. She did mention this week she went to Cornerstone. Like, the largest Christian rock festival on the planet . . .

I begin, "Hey, so, um . . . I have something I want to tell you." Stacey's blue eyes settle on mine, like a rare butterfly alighted on my finger. My heart flutters to match. Oh no, do I know anyone else in this bar? I have a look around before I spill the beans.

"So, I want to let you know that I really appreciate our chats. And I trust you. So, I need to be honest with you." I take a big exhale. And a drink. Another breath. Here goes nothing.

"I'm gay." The words hurl out of me like a fast ball. My breath is caught up in my chest with nowhere to go. I look down at my hands in my lap.

"Thanks for sharing that. That's a-okay with me," Stacey says. Every molecule of my body exhales.

"Great! I like you. I mean, as a friend," I say.

Stacey nods in agreement.

"Well, there's something I would like to tell you too," she begins. "I normally don't tell people anything. It's hard for me to open up."

I feel like I'm going to be handed a secret look into an unexplored jungle. I lean in. My eyes look up to see a pale face with eyes showing pain...and? I place my hand on hers, letting her know I'm with her. Her hand is delicate. Not rough from seasons of mom-laundry and dishes, or rough like a man's. Like polished alabaster.

Like a mouse presenting me a tiny piece of cheese, she says, "I'm gay, too."

I immediately pull back my hand. What are the fucking odds?

"*Really*?" I blurt out like I'm in cheerleading camp. This is so weird. Do gay people just have a gay-dar, even if they're in the closet? That must mean that we really aren't very good at being in the closet then. I'll have to think about that for work. My stomach tightens. Oh no, the Club.

"Thanks so much for trusting me. Does anyone at work know?" I ask.

Stacey puts her poker face back on, "No, and I need it to stay that way. For obvious reasons. Are you in the closet, too?"

I shuffle in my seat to sit on one foot, lean back and fold my arms.

"Yep."

"Has it been hard then," she asks in reply, "being married to a man who knows?"

My cheeks grow hot. With words like venom dripping from a snake's tooth I say, "*Oh, he doesn't know*. Only a couple other people and my therapist do. And hard is an understatement."

I know now is not the time to focus on Mark. I take a breath and refocus on me.

"So, I just learned I might be gay about a year ago. Actually, a friend had to tell me I might be gay. Which is pretty embarrassing. So, I've been mad at myself a bit about it. At least I know now. Better than if I found out when my boobs were saggy! **Ha**! Anyway, I didn't think I was gay until last month. I've been trying to stay married. For my kids' sake."

I hold up my drink. My cheeks have cooled, like the tide receding, "Here's to being out of the closet, in the booth."

CHAPTER 70
Her Hold

Hand of a Greek goddess,
slender, perfect,
disobedient to her
daily manual labor.
An unintentional touch -
granite, cold.
Nonetheless,
my heart, paddled awake,
grease fire in my discarded hearth.
Every hair on my body, erect,
begging for more.
Fuel.

PART SIX

THE JABBERWOCKY

CHAPTER 71

So this is how the cookie crumbles?

EVERY DAY for the next week, I feel like something is making me move a little slower, sleep longer, go to bed earlier. I start pounding unnecessarily large amounts of vitamin C into my system to get rid of whatever 'it' is. Because I need the energy to be angry at Mark.

As I turn the knob to my bedroom door, I thank God the kids went down with only two books; my voice is almost dead. I lock the guest room door behind me and melt into my bed, shaking in my fleece nightgown underneath three blankets.

A large mug of honey lemon tea steams on my side table, alongside a brick-sized stack of Kleenex and bottle of NyQuil. I feel like a caught fish, tired of flopping on the boat floor. I need help; time to call Mary.

"What the fuck is up, woman?" Mary answers.

I have no energy so I get straight to the point. I clear my throat, blow my nose.

"Mark cleared out our savings this week," I honk. There's a pause on the other end. I can feel her putting her hands on her hips.

"Why the hell would he do that?" Time to get her up to speed.

"So, he invested in a stock program at work that is supposed to guarantee money back plus a 50% return after one year. I told him *No*, but he did it anyway."

I sit up and take a sip of my tea, blow my nose. One ear is officially clogged. I put my phone to my other ear.

"So you can't get it back?"

"Nope." I reply.

"Heidi, I need to tell you something," Mary says, "and I mean this in the nicest way. You sound like shit."

I laugh and blow my nose. "Yeah, I already knew that." My voice tightens, and I take a long sip of tea.

Mary puts on her mom voice and begins, "you need to see a doctor. Your stress and this sickness are gonna kill you. Now, my dear, let's move onto something a less stressful. How about, with the last of your voice, you tell me a little about your new friend, Stacey-from-work?"

I smile.

to my husband

Fuck you
for being so small you cannot understand
*Did you know that you play the sweet goofy Dad only
when we have company?*

Fuck you
for being so small your heart only, really, cares about you.
I have the job, so I need to get some sleep.

Fuck you
for saying what you need to say to protect your
most precious asset.
We'll get all the money back + interest back in a year, I promise.

And fuck me
for not being tall enough yet
to say these things to your face.

CHAPTER 73

September 30

TWO WEEKS LATER, I am better. Not *take-over-the-world* better. But one round of antibiotics to kick my respiratory infection helped somewhat, before I broke out in hives.

And no, I didn't yell at Mark about the money. I just don't think yelling will help. Plus, my voice isn't completely back yet. I have enough energy to fight the daily battles of kids, work, and Mark. Like the battle of today. I sit in my car over lunch. I dial Mark's number and look down at a completed checklist, thumping my pen on the steering wheel.

"Yep, everything is ready for your brother and his family tonight. Beer is cold. House clean. I ironed Barbie's cheerleading outfit. The car is packed for the tailgate, obviously except ice. Pizzas are pre-ordered for dinner. As you know, I'm working late to make up sick time. So I hope to be home around nine."

Mark immediately challenges me, "You gonna finally, gonna come back and sleep with me, then?"

Silence. This is going to be the most awkward weekend. Should I sleep with Barbie or in the dining room? My body closes up like a flower at night.

"Gotta get back to work," I say. "See you later."

I pack up my things around eight. I can't work anymore, it's almost been twelve hours. I gather my things and slowly walk to my car like it's my last walk. Maybe I can hang out at the neighborhood park for an hour. Then I'll be able to go home and get the kids in bed with minimal awkwardness. Wait a minute. A new plan hatches in my brain. I zip up my fall-but-wished-it-were-a-winter coat, then get in my car, turn on the heat, defrost my hands, and text Stacey.

Me: What'cha doing right now?

Stacey: not much.

Me: I don't want to go home yet. It's gonna be awkward!

Stacey: Sorry.

Me: You up for meeting at Clark Park? I need a good swing.

Stacey: LOL, sure.

Not fifteen minutes later, we are at a local park, Clark Park. The temperature is dropping, the grass dewy. The standard playground is flanked on one side by trees, basketball courts, and tennis courts. The entire park is deserted with the exception of some demanding crows. The single squeaky swing set in the direct glow of the orange automatic lights next to the tennis courts.

The first brush of winter meets my cheeks as I pump on the swing. Stacey slides into a swing next to me and gently rocks back and forth, in jeans, her work scarf, and an unbuttoned black wool coat. She reminds me of a teenager, *just hangin' out*. I smile.

After a few minutes, I stop.

"Oh my god, my hips need a break. Hey, you wanna go and sit on the tire swing and chat? I think I have about ten minutes."

We both fit on the tire swing. Barely. I look up. My face is inches from hers. I can smell her smell. A gentle saltiness, like a breeze flitting through a transparent curtain in a seaside cabin. Stacey's eyes flash in the lamplight. Her gaze quickens my pulse. My throat goes dry.

A minute movement; I press my mouth to hers. A tender softness meets me, a ripe peach, a single rose petal, a drip of warm massage oil rolling down the back of my hand.

This. Finally. My hands grip the chains, and I lean into her. Like cascades of the softest soap bubbles roll down my full body in an almost-overheated shower. *More.*

No. Wait.

As if throwing an anchor into the ocean from a plane, I pull myself away, a giant smile grows on my lips.

"Hey," I say.

Stacey's full lips curve upward.

"Hey," she replies.

Shock, flush, surprise, heat. I am alive as a phoenix birthed from a fire. I stumble over my words,

"Well, that was, um, unexpected. And thank you."

Her clear, piercing eyes meet mine. Inches away. I feel naked, unafraid, willing to show her, tell her . . . anything.

"Thank you, too." she whispers, her lips like deep red strawberries.

My fuzzy head reminds me to check my watch. "Shit, I have to go. I just want to say that kissing you was worth waiting thirty-five years for."

I put my hands on her cheeks, her silken hair, and pull her to me again. Yes. This is me. I feel like endless rolling fields of every shade of wildflowers, where just the day before were only fallow fields.

CHAPTER 74
clark

Laying here
Dizzy.
Breathless.
Still feeling my hand in your hair,
softly swaying on the tire.
A mere hour after we parted,
I still feel you on my lips
made soft from yours,
bringing my entire world out of focus,
except for you.
Forged into view, as
my heart, around yours,
embraced her Love
for the first time.

CHAPTER 75
Walgreens

ONE WEEK LATER, I sit at my desk and stare at my "to-do" sticky note for lunch errands: Antibiotics, round two–Walgreens it is. Too bad hot toddies didn't work. The lemonade and whisky really knock me out until I get up and double dose the NyQuil.

I sit at my desk at work and close my breathing drawer. *Well, it is actually now stocked with things that help me breathe.*

I throw on my hat and scarf. Time to go. *I should have known how sick I am because I'm wearing thermals in October.*

Stacey and I climb into Miss Daisy on a compressing October day. One of those first days that fills you with winter-is-coming dread.

"You okay stopping by Walgreens before we find food?"

"Sure, anything."

I pop in a new 70s mix CD from a friend. *Earth, Wind, and Fire, Carpenters, Fleetwood Mac.* At the end is Leonard Coen's *Hallelujah,* performed by some soulful female. I skip to that song.

"*Hallelujah* is definitely my favorite song on this CD." Stacey nods in agreement.

I turn up the volume and start to drive. Through my raspiness, I start to sing. It's like my body forgets that I'm sick. Stacey then starts singing too. She's not doing exactly the notes that I am, but complementary ones.

My voice gets stronger.

I pull in and park in the Walgreens parking lot.

My anger and hope and doubt all flow from my soul, filling the small cavity of the minivan. And Stacey's voice follows mine like two pieces of satin caressing, playing with each other in a jubilant summer breeze. I look deep into her glass-blue eyes, and see a soft, brilliant light. This is Stacey.

Her voice delicately, effortlessly, completely, and resoundingly, intertwines around mine.

CHAPTER 76

Nachos

TWO FRENZIED WEEKS LATER, I hand a staple gun up to Stacey. She came over today in jeans, rolled-up green camp shirt, and a light brown backwards wool flat cap—apparently that used to be her grandpa's. The heat between us is growing. Even as she climbed up the step ladder and stapled colorful sheets from Goodwill onto the basement ceiling for my daughter's fourth birthday Mad Hatter's Tea Party, I couldn't help but think there's nothing sexier than someone helping me with parenting shit.

"Thanks for doing this. It would have been a hell of a week without you." I say, my gratitude overflowing. Stacey triggers the staple the gun for the last sheet, her strong, flexed forearms drawing my gaze.

"No problem. I think you may have outdone yourself," she says as she climbs down the ladder.

I look around the basement. Wonderland. The rainbow of sheets draws my gaze. A hand-painted pin-the-smile-on-the-vanishing-cat, a corner to pretend to play cards, and a stuffed white rabbit to play catch the rabbit. My crowning achievement is the tea table. Over the last month, I raided Goodwill for a plethora of mismatched tea kettles and cups.

The world's lowest–and longest–tea table is ready, set for twenty-five.

"I'm gonna change, check on food, and get Jonathan and Barbie ready. You good?" I ask.

"Yep, I'll wait down here," Stacey replies.

I bound upstairs and whip on my non-slutty Alice costume. Yep, it took me over a month to find a costume appropriate for outside of the bedroom. Next is my least favorite part of all family events, doing Barbie's hair. After the usual hair-curling screams, Barbie, now Tinkerbell, is ready for her party. A couple minutes later I have Jonathan dressed as an adorable Captain Hook.

One child for each hand, we walk downstairs. The kids pull me forward with excitement. *I haven't let them see the basement all week.* We hear the laughter of a crowd emanating from the basement. Friends have already arrived.

Before going downstairs I fill my snack tray, say hi to some incoming guests, and then I herd the kids toward the basement stairs. And that's when I see him. Mark. Just sitting on the couch. After spending the past month on this party, he finds time to just sit there? I decide to remind him of his duty.

"You good with the nachos for the upstairs crowd?" I say, clenching my teeth. Mark nods to me and raises his drink from the recliner.

"Check. I will handle nacho distribution and college football for everyone top-side," he confirms. Never any more than is asked of him. Never any extra offer of help. Never safe. Never again.

I juggle the tray and open the basement door to let the kids run down. Rising squeals of delight amplify the dissonance I feel. My fists clench the sides of the tray. I close my eyes. I can only see his hand, shaking his mixed drink, ice cubes chest-bumping for his win. My loss. My subservience to this role, his life. I feel some off-centered remark erupting, like *need a sippy cup for that?* I steady my tongue.

I move to the bottom of the stairs, still heated. At least 40 people are in my basement, waiting. My flashing eyes scan the crowd, and land on Stacey's. She smiles her curtained smile, her heart-shaped strawberry lips slightly curved. The sight envelops me like new bed sheets, cooling, smoothing over my heat. Focus, Heidi. You have work to do. Save it for later.

CHAPTER 77
Alice

I have decided I shall believe up to six impossible things before breakfast.

One: I am fearfully and wonderfully made.
Two: I am made of feelings, titanium, and butterfly wings.
Three: God is with me. My Earth Mother is with me.
Four: I am molting from hardly myself to almost myself to always myself. And back again.
Five: I have friends, but I am the Champion of my life.
Six: The jabberwocky is deadly, and I can defeat it.

CHAPTER 78

Later

ALL THE PARTYGOERS HAVE LEFT. The kids are happily in their own Wonderland, dreamland. I go upstairs and change out of Alice into a tracksuit. My trusty pair of Spanx lays tossed on my bed, and I pause. You are great for my waist, but no longer good for my life. I smile.

Before leaving my room, I decide to keep Alice's black ribbon in my pixie hair. A little bit of her.

I walk downstairs. All the lights in the house are off, except the solitary one over the kitchen table. Only the drone of the ESPN announcers remains; college football is still on.

My anger is right below the surface. *Ready for my Jabberwocky.*

Mark is standing when he meets me, with a puffed chest. Waiting for me. His eyes dark, like black oil, covering up his own turmoil. He is gripping another almost-empty rum and coke. Ready for some satisfaction from blowing off some steam.

Sorry Charlie, I am no longer your punching bag.

"So, what the hell is your problem today? You've been avoiding me. And now that you are always hanging out with

Mary, I'm taking a back seat. You are always gone, texting, hanging out with work people. What the fuck is going on?"

"I want a divorce," I say.

"You *what*?" he yells.

"I want a divorce. I'm done." I walk the words out like a turtle.

Speaking the words floods every molecule of my body with strength, like I am made of giant, green, flexible vines that laugh in hurricanes. I can take anything. Then I feel an encompassing embrace. A presence. Mary, Stacey, Kevin, my friends, my parents. Like when Harry Potter got that extra energy in his wand from all those people who were dead when he had to take on Voldemort.

I am calm, ready to die, to live, for me, for my kids. For our happiness.

I sit down at the table with a tall back.

CHAPTER 79

endings

So, this is the end.
You have crossed the bridge I crossed.
Branded me quitter, abuser,
one-who-thinks-she-is-entitled-to-your-money
without living with you,
trying to be close to you,
have sex with you.
Well, fuck you.
I've dealt too long
with your *second-to-none*
absent-fucking feelings.
(Except for, of course,
when you lash out.)
Treating us as possessions, pets.
Waking up each morning,
tails wagging, to see
if we were good puppies.
But we never were.

It's now time
that you felt
how it feels
to be left
all alone
in the store.

CHAPTER 80

The Business Card

FIVE HOURS OF ACCUSATIONS and three hours of
fitful sleep later, I rub open my dry, stinging eyes. Alice
make-up still crusty. I bet I look rough today. Alice's black
hair ribbon is on my bedside table. I tie it around my wrist.

Wow. I said it, multiple times. "I want a divorce. I do
not trust you. I no longer love you." I was calm. And I didn't
back down.

Other thoughts start to swim. My stomach is acid
empty; I need some quiet and coffee before Jonathan
wakes. He's earlier than a rooster.

I drag my heavy feet into my wool socks and push my
arms clumsily into my robe, then unlock my bedroom door.

In the kitchen, I fill up Mr. Coffee and stare out of our
small sink window. The sky is under an uneven blanket of
fluffy clouds and the sun is peeking one eye from behind a
neighbor's roof, flooding my torso with warmth, light, hope.
A bright hand offering a new day. The first day of my new
life. A small smile pulls on my lips.

I didn't hide. Or smooth over his anger, Spanx-style. I
didn't tell him about being gay. But that's not his business.
Anymore.

My stomach sinks. Shit. What am I going to do **now**? I have to live here in his angry steam bath until I can figure out another place. How will I manage?

I turn on Mr. Coffee and shuffle over to the kitchen table.

As I pull out my chair something catches my eye, a sky-blue business card on the floor underneath. *Well, that wasn't there three hours ago.* I pick it up. It reads:

Hello,

this is God.

I'll be handling all of your problems today.

Have a miraculous day.

I melt down on the floor, sitting, leaning on a table leg. The tears toboggan-slide out. Mr. Coffee beeps. I feel like a brand-new chick. Blind and helpless, held and loved. Thank you, God.

I hear little plodding feet and wipe my eyes.

"Mommy, why are you sitting on the floor?" my son asks.

"I found a special card today sweetheart. Want some breakfast?"

CHAPTER 81

Found

It's time I found my heart today,
because it's time to mend my heart.
And when my love loses me,
I weigh her beating ache,
because I have felt my heart.

It's time I heard my soul today,
because it's time to know my Self.
And when I don't take knock or call,
Dear Friend, but first,
I'm trying to hear my
big, beautiful, lesbian, divorcing momma
soul.

Potty break

Yeah! You made it all the way through! You deserve a potty break! And don't forget to get yourself some chippies or M&Ms as a reward.

While you are munching, are you ready to start *Peeling Your Onion*? That's the companion self-help workbook that takes you through the exact process I went through in this book to find my inner onions and speak up for my joy. What does it include? The *Peeling Your Onion* and *The Feelings Parfait* exercises plus two other exercises called *But First, Friends* and *The Stepstool of Support*. Pinky promise it will get you on the path to unlocking more authentic joy in your life. How about I throw in my family's Swedish meatball recipe? Even if you are a mostly veggie-saurus like me, I provide alternatives to the meat. Search for *Peeling Your Onion* on Amazon today!

Personal Ads
(aka The Acknowledgements)

I have a confession. I usually skim through the acknowledgements. Because *I don't know* the people. So, welcome to The Personal Ads. Most folks are mentioned here, some with headshots. Grab a drink and get to know these awesome souls.

Those who were there

An unending thanks to those who supported me during the journey I shared in this story.

To Kevin and Mary, thank you for your patience and guidance while I wandered down and around many rabbit holes. And thank you for giving me the space to explore who I was, knowing I was loved, no matter what.

To my preschool mom friends at Barbie's Fourth Birthday party: Katrina, Martina, Maria, Colleen, Christine, Rachel, and Amy. Thank you for loving me as the Alice I was and Alice I was becoming.

And to Jeanette. I met Jeanette at church during the time of my book. A dozen years later, she is still one of my best friends. This quilter extraordinaire gave me my first Melody Beattie book and is a big, steady mama-bear in my life. I am blessed by your steady love.

Writing Mentors: the big shots

Jeff Goins, Bestselling Author, Speaker, Writing Coach. Jeff's love and gift of helping writers helped me dream, start, and build my online home of HeidiEsther.com. I am forever grateful. His little empire can be found at goinswriter.com.

Dawn Montefusco, Transformational Writing Coach www.DawnMontefusco.com. Dawn's NorthWest-coast rockstar love, in the form of a course, called One Short Book (OSB), kept my ass writing until I was done. Courage, compassion, and consistency might just be my first tat. *From Dawn: My life's mission is to help men and women over 40 break through resistance and be creative and write! I*  *like to waste my time by watching well-written TV shows, such as Lucifer, The Queens Gambit, and Ted Lasso. I want to be reincarnated as my dog Morris.*

Book Magicians

Kathryn Brown "Kathy" Ramsparger, Award-winning Author, Coach, and Speaker. https://groundonecoaching. com, https://twitter.com/kramsperger, https://facebook. com/kathyramsperger, https://linktr.ee/kathyramsperger, Kathy is a gentle, curious, patient writing coach. She worked with me 1:1, helped me define my worldview, and zero in on the purpose of this book. *From Kathy: I want to be reincarnated as a female explorer or anthropologist, like Amelia Earhart. My greatest achievement is raising two* *decent kids while working & writing award-winning books. My deceased BFF (and whispering Muse) Stacey Waller still knows me best.*

Sarah D. Moore, Freelance Editor and Proofreader. *Sarah@bloomingwriter.com* Sarah helped me boil down and

dialog up this book. She was honest, direct, exacting, thoughtful, kind, and encouraging. The whole package. I found her at upwork.com. *From Sarah: My life's mission is to deplete the world's supply of seafood and champagne. I like to waste my time staring at the trees outside my office window. An important part of my morning is checking the online papers for editing errors.*

Gentiana Keka, Professional Designer gentiana.keka.5 on Facebook Designed the book cover.

She was positive, creative, responsive, and an overall delight to work with. Found her on upwork.com via the handle KS BOY. *From Gentania: My life mission, for the moment, is to grow up and educate my 3-year-old daughter! I waste time with her, play with her, and do everything with her.*

Shabbir Hussain, Print+eBook wizard, top-rated plus on Upwork. Shabbir patiently walked

this first-time author through the entire book and ebook creation process. *From Shabbir: My life's mission is to publish a few best-selling books. I want to be reincarnated as an invisible being. You can always bribe me with your pleasant smile.*

Denis Rykov, Audiobook producer, stellercradleprod@ gmail.com Thank you for sharing your meticulous Zone of Genius with the world. *From Denis: An important part of my morning is to stare thoughtlessly at the sky for a moment. You can always bribe me with a sensitive conversation. The lesson I learned from my greatest failure was there is always more to learn.*

Stephanie Treasure, Online Marketing Strategist and Business Mentor StephanieTreasure.com. While not a book-wizard, Stephanie helped me gain courage and visibility to show up and move forward with this book. I was in her 90-day online visibility boot camp, called the V.I.P. Accelerator. Stephanie was thoughtful, inspiring, and practical!  *From Stephanie: An important part of my morning is prayer, meditation and affirmations. One of my favorite games as a child was hide and seek. My life's mission is to help as many women as possible to run a successful business that allows them to live the life of their dreams.*

Book Launch: Team Sunshine

Many thanks to Book Launch **Team Sunshine!** I am truly, madly, deeply grateful to the family and friends who helped these pages shine their newborn light. I am blessed to be in your orbit, always.

Storytelling and Writing Friends

To Kris, Deb, Marla, Patty, Jane, and Kay. Thank you for being my That's My Story CU_storytelling friends the past six years. It was terrifying and exhilarating to speak my truth to live people the first time. But, with your support and love, I never looked back. Or shut up. ;)

To my Shut up And Write(c) Tuesday morning group: Starla, Diana, Cope, Louise, Amy, Eva, Emily, and Laurie. Thanks for being so welcoming to a wacky green grammatically-indifferent writer.

To my *One Short Book* Accountability Group, thank you for showing up weekly to make sure I was not distracting myself with reorganizing my linen closet. **Catherine Chapey,** keep listening. **Ameena Lacy-Viet,** no other words than You Rock, woman! **Dale Walsh,** Mental Health Coach & Poet. dalewalsh.com *From Dale: My life's mission is to eliminate stigma of psychic affect ("mental illness"). I want to be reincarnated as the next Derek Jeter. People always ask me about my Poetry.* **Marilyn Mercado,** Yoga, Dance, Fitness Instructor Wise Warrior NO KA OI Group *From Marilyn: My life's mission is to share my gift of healing others thru yoga, movement, and my book. An important part of my morning is being out in nature and being grateful. The lesson I learned from my greatest failure was be honest, truthful, and listen to my intuition.*

My (Pandemic) Sanity Buddies

Tori Beach, Videographer toribeach.com Tori is the little sister I never had. She keeps me inspired (and thankful to be a dog mom!) that I can help ignite and awaken other souls to self-love and joy in my unique way. *From Tori: My life's*

mission is to help tell other people's stories through the art of video. I like to waste my time by watching DIY and home decor videos on Youtube. An important part of my morning is coffee... what can I say?

David Hibbs, Director of Development, Forest Ridge Academy *Picture name:* David Hibbs was the perfect friend to have in the pandemic. A fellow fundraising professional, he reminded me of all the knowledge and wisdom I accrued in my seventeen years in small, underpaid, under-acknowledged non-profits. He lifted me in a way no-one else did in my previous seventeen years. I am forever

grateful. *From David: You can always bribe me with chocolate-covered cherries. My greatest achievements are raising two wonderful children and enjoying life with my wife Maria. The lessons I learned from my failures are to take ownership for them and always move forward.*

Leslie Kimble, Artist and Musician Leslie was my weekly walking buddy while I wrote this. We verbally processed midwestern motherhood, social injustices, and plant-based food in the pandemic, even at below zero temps. Yes, we were that desperate. *From Leslie: My life's mission is to encourage others and create meaningful, thought-provoking art and music. An important part of my*

morning is Yoga, meditation, reading and journaling. You can always bribe me with ice cream, chocolate or wine. Or sour candy.

My Fam To my parents, Barb and Hal, who taught me to not quit when things get tough. And that my heart is strong enough to accomplish anything, whether it is cheerleading, divorcing, cooking, or foraging a new mid-life path. I love you.

To **Jonathan**, my sweetheart. Thank you for giving me the gift of motherhood. Your love and kindness, and the fact I could always find you behind my knee, was a north star that taught me noone should be left behind. Including myself.

To **Barbie**, my Shero. Thank you for always staying true to you and taking on your own Jabberwockys. Your ferocity of spirit and self-love has shown me that my 12 years of growth and healing has already had a ripple effect, in a miraculous way. I am always proud of you.

To **Stacey**, the unexpected love of my life. Thank you for wading into deep waters with me. Thank you for opening my door to joy. To our blessed, messy, wacky life. And thank you for being my rock through divorce, codependency, depression, anxiety, unemployment, a pandemic, teenagers and writing. You have so many punches on your ticket to heaven, babe. Thanks for believing in me before I knew how.

Hang on

Thank you for reading my book!
I really appreciate all of your feedback, and
I love hearing what you have to say!

I need your input to the next version of this book, and
my future stories, even better.

Please leave me a helpful review on Amazon letting
me know what you thought of the book.

With love, light, laughter, and gratitude for you,

Heidi Esther

About the author

Heidi Esther is a storyteller, poet, big-feeler, midwestern momma, and spoiler of all dogs, especially her chestnut-eyed Olive. *She guides fellow soul-searchers to greater Joy and Authenticity with her practical + playful Mindfulness + Resilience Tools.* Yes, exactly like this story and her companion workbook.

She resides in Central Illinois with her <u>prankster wife, two eye-rolling teenagers, and two spoiled dogs.</u> When she doesn't have her head in the clouds or a motivational book, she can be found trying to teach her children the virtues of meditation, making sourdough pancakes, or growing parsley for caterpillars.

Are you ready to take a journey to your Joyfully Ever After? Then Heidi Esther, your new best non-preachy mom friend, is here to walk with you and give you the tools you need to unlock your authentic Joy. What are the tools? Relatable true stories, playful printables, empowering conversations, and self-reflections.

All designed with one goal in mind. To guide you to your Joyfully Ever After! Are you ready? Get your free JumpStart to Joy guide today at heidiesther.com/joy + Join her *My Joyfully Ever After* Group on Facebook! Claim *your joy* starting now.

Would you like a FREE slice of self-love and joy?

Grab your Self-Love Story Bundle!
(Funny Story + Playful printable + Delicious Recipe)
Go to https://heidiesther.com/bookbundle1 and grab it!

Made in the USA
Las Vegas, NV
28 April 2022